Clouds, Acharnians, Lysistrata

A Companion to the Penguin translation of
Alan H. Sommerstein by

Sir Kenneth Dover
and
Simon Tremewan

Bristol Classical Press

First published in 1989 by
Bristol Classical Press
an imprint of
Gerald Duckworth & Co. Ltd
The Old Piano Factory
48 Hoxton Square, London N1 6PB

Reprinted 1992

A catalogue record for this book is available
from the British Library

ISBN 1-85399-054-X

Printed in Great Britain by
Booksprint, Bristol

Preface

This commentary on three plays of Aristophanes is designed for readers who do not know any Greek but wish to understand more of Aristophanes than they can learn simply from a translation and a few pages of footnotes.

We assume that the reader is using the Penguin translation by Professor Alan Sommerstein (*Aristophanes: Lysistrata, The Achamians, The Clouds*, Harmondsworth 1973), and references are given in accordance with the page numbers of that translation, not the numbering of verses within the plays. The translation is rather free, sometimes replacing Greek idiom and humour by analogous British idiom and humour, and sometimes omitting the technical, topical, literary and mythological allusions which are abundant in Aristophanes. It may be felt that to cut so much in translating a comedy is rather like serving up a pudding from which most of the raisins have been removed; but that, after all, is what one would do for a guest who could not digest raisins.

We have been sparing of comment on the words of the Greek text, and we have been careful not to turn what should be a commentary on the content of the play into a nit-picking commentary on the accuracy or appropriateness of the translation. There are a few places, but only a few, where we have felt obliged to express disagreement with Professor Sommerstein over the translation of a phrase. On stage-directions, see p. x.

Kenneth Dover
St Andrews

Simon Tremewan
Sherborne

Contents

Introduction

Aristophanes' career as a comic dramatist lasted from 427 to 387 BC. He was a contemporary of Socrates and Thucydides, a generation younger than Sophocles and Euripides, and a generation older than Plato.

He put on at least forty plays, of which eleven survived into the Middle Ages and so to our own times; we know the rest only from a few papyrus fragments and many quotations from them by later writers.

Plays were produced at Athens at two festivals, the City Dionysia (in spring) and the Lenaea (in winter). Tragedy was an ingredient of these festivals from the late sixth century BC onwards; comedy was included in the City Dionysia from early in the fifth century, and in the Lenaea from the middle of that century. Comic dramatic performance 'on the fringe' – unscripted, which does not mean unrehearsed – may have been very much older than that.

Drama in the Greek world was a genre of poetry, and a comedy, like a tragedy, comprised both dialogue in verse, spoken by the characters, and lyrics sung by a chorus. The chorus-leader also took some part in the dialogue, and on occasion an individual character sang. The chorus was an indispensable ingredient of the play; it was from the chorus that the play commonly took its title (*Acharnians* and *Clouds* are examples, *Lysistrata* an exception), its central importance was a significant constraint on the imagination of the dramatist when he devised the 'plot', and in some plays (again, *Acharnians* and *Clouds* are good examples) there comes a point in the middle at which the characters are off-stage, the 'dramatic illusion' is partially ruptured, and the chorus addresses the audience directly (the *parabasis*).

This was no doubt a formal feature of the genre which Aristophanes inherited – and was free, in the course of time, to modify, as we see particularly from his last two plays, *Women in Assembly* and *Wealth*. Another inherited feature was the *agon*, 'contest', a set-piece debate between two opponents, in which the chorus 'holds the ring'; *Clouds* contains two such contests, between Right and Wrong (pp. 149-57) and between Strepsiades and his son (pp. 166-72), and *Lysistrata* one (pp. 199-205). The formal framework is absent from Dikaiopolis' speech of self-justification to the chorus and from his triumph over Lamachus (*Acharnians*, pp. 71-6), but three years later it reasserts itself in *Wasps*, where Bdelykleon is in a situation very similar to that of Dikaiopolis. This fact reminds us that although we are justified in speaking of 'traditional features' in Aristophanic comedy, the Athenians' reception of comedy was not so hidebound that a poet could not innovate except by one cautious step at a time.

The same can be said of the subject-matter of comedy. Some of Aristophanes' plays are devoted to the ridicule and vilification of individual contemporaries (*Knights, Clouds*); and others (*Acharnians, Lysistrata*) are about contemporary issues on which the assembly could take decisions; others again (*Wasps*, and to some extent *Women in Assembly* and *Wealth*) satirize and criticise contemporary attitudes and ways of behaving; while *Frogs* and, to some extent, *Women at the Thesmophoria* are about poetry, and *Peace* and *Birds* are fantasies which do not fit easily into any of those categories (*Peace* was produced after the decision to make peace had been taken). Some comedies were burlesque versions of myths which other genres of poetry treated seriously; we know that Aristophanes wrote some such burlesques, but they do not happen to have survived.

It is not easy, therefore, to define the 'essence' of Aristophanic comedy, beyond making the obvious point that it was designed to provoke laughter and not to instil grief. Nor is it easy to give a concise answer to the question which the modern reader most often asks: did the poet seriously intend, using ridicule and absurdity as a means to an end, to affect the behaviour of his fellow-citizens and cause them to take particular political decisions? Being himself a citizen, Aristophanes is likely to have held strong opinions on many political issues, and it would be surprising if he wrote in such a way as to convey the impression that those opinions were ridiculous or discreditable. At the same time, he was, like all dramatists at the festivals, competing for a prize, and self-interest would deter him from going blatantly against sentiments and attitudes which were widespread at the time of writing, except in so far as Greek tradition accorded a poet the right to upbraid his fellow-citizens in general terms for their follies and weaknesses. On more specific issues predominant sentiments change with circumstances, and it is prudent to treat the problem of the 'serious intention' of each play separately.

One thing, however, can be said with assurance about Aristophanic comedy as a whole: like fairy-tales, it accommodates the supernatural and the fantastic, and it is always free to disregard the constraints of cause and effect in real life. In *Peace* the principal character fattens up a dung-beetle so that he can fly up to heaven on its back and bring the goddess Peace back to earth; in *Birds* a similarly enterprising character persuades the birds to build a fortified city in the sky and blockade the gods. We are not allowed to ask '*How* could that be done?' – nor 'How could representatives of states at war with Athens come in safety to Lysistrata's meeting or Dikaiopolis' market?' On occasion, inconsistencies at the heart of the plot are tolerated; thus the complaint of the women in *Lysistrata* is that their husbands are never at home, but the sex-strike they envisage as the remedy for that situation is effective only because the men *are* at home. Comic situations proceed in temporal sequence, but the causal sequences leave loose ends, and the dramatist can choose to concentrate on one aspect of a situation at a time.

The plays were produced in the open air, in daylight, and in a theatre which had no stage-curtains. When we have to imagine action – such as the opening scene of *Clouds* – as taking place in the dark, the words of the text make that clear to us. Action which we must imagine as taking place inside a building – and this too is true of the opening scene of *Clouds* – in fact has to take place outside. Occasionally, as when Strepsiades brings his bed out of the school, action which most naturally belongs to the interior of a building is quite deliberately and explicitly transferred to the outside.

The acting area consisted of a circular dancing-floor (the *orchestra*), round half of which (or a bit more than half) the audience sat in concentric semicircles. Beyond the perimeter of the other half was a rectangular stage-building with at least one central door, and probably two other doors, facing the audience. The area along the front of this building was higher than the orchestra by one or two steps. The orchestra was entered from each side by a broad passage-way (*parodos*) between the end of the stage-building and the end of the area occupied by the audience.

The actors wore masks which wholly concealed their facial expressions from the audience, so that emotion could be shown only by words, gesture and bodily movement. All parts, male and female alike, were taken by men, and for comic effect those taking male parts very commonly wore large artificial genitals and padding to give them big paunches.

The texts of plays in ancient times carried no stage-directions, and they were also deficient in indicating changes of speaker and the identity of speakers; critics, from the third century BC onwards, have therefore rightly considered all such matters as open to discussion. The stage-directions inserted in the translation to which the commentaries refer amount to suggestions for production of the play in a modern theatre. In so far as they affect scenery and divisions of the acting area, they must on no account be taken as statements of what happened in the ancient Athenian theatre. As for comic 'business', the translator's directions could sometimes be right – indeed, they could often be right – but it must be remembered that they are modern interpretation and not laid down by the author himself (see pp. 36 ff. of the translator's introduction).

Down to the invention of printing in the fifteenth century, texts were transmitted entirely by manual copying, and from the very beginning copyists made mistakes. As the Roman Empire became increasingly Christian, people's interest in pagan plays gradually diminished, and in the end only a few manuscripts, containing only a few plays, survived into the Middle Ages. The Byzantine manuscripts on which printed editions ultimately depend were all derived from those few. Now and again an editor has to choose between alternative readings presented by the manuscripts, and sometimes, when no manuscript makes sense, he has to 'emend', i.e. decide what it seems to him the author probably wrote. This is not a modern complication; even in the author's lifetime a reader sometimes had to ask himself whether the text in front of him was corrupt. In the few cases in the plays in this volume where a textual problem really matters to the sense, attention will be drawn to it in the commentaries.

Most medieval manuscripts of Aristophanes are full of marginal notes ('scholia') which constitute a commentary. Some of these notes are medieval in origin, but many can be shown to have originated in the ancient world between the third century BC and the fifth century AD; hence the occasional references to 'ancient commentators'.

CLOUDS

Aristophanes produced his first play in 427 BC. *Clouds* was his fifth, produced in the spring of 423. To his great disappointment – and for reasons which we do not know – it was not well received. He set about revising it, but abandoned the process of revision about 418. This incompletely revised version, which was never put on stage, is the play which we have.

The play concerns an old farmer, Strepsiades, who married a wife from a social class above his own. Their son, Pheidippides, encouraged by his mother, has got his father into debt by associating with young men devoted to horse-riding and chariot-racing. Strepsiades wonders how he can escape his debts, because his creditors are threatening to sue him. He has heard that certain professional teachers of a new kind ('sophists') can, in return for a fee, teach a man how to win lawsuits even when in the wrong, and he thinks of sending Pheidippides to learn this dishonest art from Socrates. Since the young man refuses, Strepsiades himself goes to the 'school' of Socrates and persuades Socrates to admit him as a pupil. He proves, however, so muddle-headed and forgetful that Socrates eventually expels him. This time, Pheidippides sulkily agrees to go and enrol in the school. On completion of the course Pheidippides returns home a different man: cynical, jaunty and dexterous in manipulating clever arguments. Strepsiades, full of joyful confidence, insults and enrages two creditors who come to demand their money. But Pheidippides has learned to despise all traditional morality, and has no hesitation in assaulting his father when they disagree over their preferences in poetry. Strepsiades, unable to defeat his son in argument and realising that his last state is worse than his first, sets fire to the school of Socrates and chases away the philosopher and his pupils with blows and missiles.

The play takes its name from the chorus of Clouds who arrive in response to Socrates' invocation after Strepsiades has first presented himself at the school. Greek intellectuals had for a long time interested themselves in the phenomena of the heavens, and Socrates in the play declares that 'the Void, the Clouds and the Tongue' are the only gods he recognises and worships. It is also not uncommon in Greek to use words such as 'cloud' and 'smoke' of illusory visions and empty talk. The Clouds encourage Strepsiades to learn from Socrates, but at the end of the play, when Strepsiades blames them for his misfortunes, they reveal themselves as true deities who have led him to disaster as a punishment for his dishonest intentions.

It is hard for us, who usually make the acquaintance of Socrates first through the pages of Plato, not to think of him as the serene but resolute old man of the *Apology*, *Crito* and *Phaedo*. We have to remind ourselves that when Aristophanes first produced *Clouds* Socrates was only 46 and had taken a strenuous part in the battle of Delium a few months earlier. We should therefore think of Socrates in the play as younger than Strepsiades.

It is even harder for us to reconcile the Socrates of the play with the Socrates whom Plato and Xenophon present. Aristophanes' Socrates is a self-confident intellectual interested in all the natural and physical sciences as well as in grammar and metre, teaching the tricks of the lawcourts for payment, denying the existence of Zeus and ridiculing the traditional gods. The Socrates of Plato and Xenophon disclaims special knowledge and is scrupulous in religious observance, tireless in his search for philosophical proof of traditional moral values, virtually devoid of curiosity about the material world and fundamentally hostile to the exploitation of political and rhetorical techniques. It has been suggested, on the strength of Socrates' admission in *Phaedo* 96A that he had once been anxious to learn about causation in the physical world, that Aristophanes presents us with Socrates as he was in the 420s, whereas Plato and Xenophon give us Socrates as he had become by the time they knew him. That passage of *Phaedo*, however, does not go far to bridge the gulf. We have to choose: either Aristophanes misrepresents Socrates, or Plato misrepresents Socrates in making him say (*Apology* 19CD):

> You yourselves saw in Aristophanes' play a 'Socrates' going around saying he was 'walking the air' and a lot more nonsense about things of which I haven't the faintest inkling...Most of you, the jury, can testify to that, and I ask all those of you who have ever heard me talk to tell one another whether anyone has ever heard me say one solitary word on any such subjects.

The most probable resolution of this conflict is the hypothesis that Aristophanes deliberately exploited for comic purposes the view taken by the plain Attic farmer of intellectuals who pursued silly, boring questions about things which are 'of no use' and, more disturbingly, subjected traditional practices, assumptions and beliefs to rational scrutiny. There were people in Aristophanes' time who studied the heavenly bodies and the weather and tried to explain them in terms of scientific laws; people who analysed language and style and formulated techniques of persuasive speaking; and people who denied the existence of gods, offered cynical views of the origins of law and argued that right and wrong were illusory. All these characteristics, as seen through the eyes of the man in the village street, are put together in a recipe which Aristophanes labels 'Socrates'. Whereas the most famous intellectuals of the period, such as Protagoras and Prodicus, were foreigners who visited Athens from time to time, Socrates was a native Athenian, the 'intellectual in residence', so to speak, known as the associate of some very prominent Athenian families; for that reason he was a suitable target for a comic poet who wished to exploit popular ideas about intellectuals. And we must not lose sight of the very unpleasant possibility – essentially similar to the explanation offered by medieval commentators on the play – that some influential friend of Aristophanes was a political enemy of an influential friend (e.g. Alcibiades) of Socrates, and that Aristophanes accepted the Greek moral principle of 'helping one's friends and harming one's enemies'.

But was it 'harm', or was it just fun? In his *Symposium*, written a few years after Aristophanes' death, Plato portrays Socrates and Aristophanes as guests of Agathon at the same dinner-party; and although they disagree deeply on the subject (love) which is discussed at the party, they do not quarrel, and Plato's presentation of Aristophanes is not malicious. Whether or not there ever was such a party (and the element of fiction in Plato should not be underestimated), it seems that by the time he wrote *Symposium* Plato had shifted from the view he took some years earlier in the *Apology*. There (18CD) he puts into the mouth of Socrates the argument that *Clouds* contributed significantly to the suspicion and ill feeling which in the end brought Socrates to trial and execution. That would not in itself be inconsistent with the possibility that a play conceived at the time as a joke could in retrospect be seen as reckless and thoughtless. There are, however, other considerations. Socrates' teaching generates in Pheidippides not trivial errors of taste, but crimes which undermined Greek society and were widely believed to merit eternal punishment in the underworld: contempt for oaths, and striking one's parents. The destruction of Socrates' house and the cry 'At 'em! Stone them!' at the end of the play are not just the reaction of a crude and angry old man, but should remind us of the massacre of Pythagoreans and burning of their houses in South Italy a generation earlier. It was a proud Athenian tradition that in 480, when the Persian invasion threatened Greece and one citizen advocated submission, his fellow-citizens burst the bonds of law in spontaneous indignation and stoned him and his family to death.

At the end of *Frogs*, produced in 405, the ghost of Aeschylus has defeated the ghost of Euripides in a contest for the throne of poetry in the underworld. The verdict of the chorus on the outcome is that tragedy in the hands of Euripides has lost its appeal because it has become infected by 'idle talk with Socrates'. This does not amount to an allegation that Euripides and Socrates were friends (though maybe they were) but expresses a conviction, not uncommon among gifted creative writers, that intellectual analysis and philosophical or scientific enquiry are hostile to the arts. How far Aristophanes shared the plain man's view (by no means peculiar to ancient Greece) that such analysis and enquiry must necessarily also undermine morality, integrity and decency is peculiarly hard to decide. It was profitable for him, as a comic poet, to adopt the coarsely conservative, philistine standpoint of male, middle-aged, middle-class Athenians at a period when unfamiliar ideas in the arts, science and philosophy were fermenting. This standpoint may have been congenial to him, as well as profitable. Some intellectuals certainly did subvert morality. Some gifted and ambitious young men who were friends and patrons of Socrates were impatient of traditional values and assumptions. Aristophanes' first play, *Banqueters*, had contained a contest between a good young man who knew his Homer and a bad young man who had a precocious interest in the techniques of the lawcourts. The cliché of thought 'old ways good, new ways bad' is a thread running through all Aristophanes' work.

ACHARNIANS

Dikaiopolis waits for the assembly. Forced to abandon his farm in the Attic countryside because of the invasions of the Peloponnesian army, he longs for peace. However, his hopes are dashed when the assembly show themselves hostile to any such suggestion by their removal of Amphitheus (who claims to speak personally for the gods and to be their agent for peace) and their continued negotiations for support from Persia and Thrace. The business of the assembly illustrates that some are profiting from the war, being sent as ambassadors at great expense to the state and large financial gain for themselves. This is a criticism which is repeated of Lamachus later in the play. By contrast Dikaiopolis, who represents the farming folk, wishes for peace and the opportunity to enjoy the countryside again. Despairing of his fellow citizens, Dikaiopolis sends Amphitheus to Sparta to make for him a personal peace. The peace which he brings back is in the form of wine (the Greek word *sponde* can be used of a 'treaty' or of a 'libation'). Wine and peace are closely associated here and throughout the play. Peace will mean the ending of the yearly Spartan invasions and the destruction of the vines. It will mean that the country festivals can once again be properly celebrated. Hence Dikaiopolis now goes to make preparations for the celebration of the rural Dionysia.

The inhabitants of the deme of Acharnae, the largest Attic deme and that which had been particularly hard pressed by the invasions of the Peloponnesians, were foremost in demanding revenge (Thuc. II 21.3). The chorus of this play consists of Acharnians. Having heard of a traitor who has made peace with the Spartans, they have come to seek him out and stone him as he leads his family in a procession celebrating the Country Dionysia. Dikaiopolis protects himself by taking hostage a charcoal basket (charcoal being a major product of the region of Acharnae and conveniently representative of the inhabitants' fiery hostility). This is a parody of a scene from Euripides' *Telephus*, where the beggar Telephus enters the Greek camp at Troy and seizes Agamemnon's son. In order to argue his case for the fruitlessness of war more persuasively, Dikaiopolis decides to go and see Euripides in order to acquire from him the rags of Telephus. Suitably attired, he argues that the war was begun for no good reason and therefore should now be stopped. Half the chorus are convinced, but the remainder call upon their champion Lamachus to represent them. This prominent young commander of the time is accused by Dikaiopolis of fuelling the war for his own gain and is scathingly mocked. The chorus are won over by Dikaiopolis' foolery. Having established his own market, to which enemy nations are welcome, Dikaiopolis receives his first customer who is from Megara. Extremely hard pressed by the effects of the war (if not the Megarian Decree, see below and note on pp. 72-3) he comes to sell his daughters in the guise of piglets. Before he can trade with this man, Dikaiopolis must drive off an informer who threatens to expose the illegal transactions. When another visitor arrives at the market, this time from Boeotia, Dikaiopolis has the sudden inspiration to sell him what was in plentiful supply at Athens, an informer.

The time has now come for the Anthesteria (earlier Dikaiopolis had celebrated the Rural Dionysia). Now others want to share Dikaiopolis' enjoyment of the benefits of peace. First a farmer whose cattle have been seized by the Boeotians, then a best man and a bridesmaid. Dikaiopolis will not share his private gain except with the bride on whose behalf the bridesmaid had appealed, since, being a woman, she 'does not deserve to suffer from the war' (pp. 97-8). A messenger arrives to summon Lamachus to duty on the borders of Attica, closely followed by another who invites Dikaiopolis to a feast with the priest of Dionysus. In the preparations that follow, peace and war are contrasted. Simultaneously Dikaiopolis prepares for feasting; Lamachus for war. After a brief choral interlude we see the two returning from their respective activities. Lamachus is wounded and supported by two slaves; Dikaiopolis is drunk and in the arms of two girls.

The modern reader on first discovering Aristophanes may often be surprised by the licence granted by the Athenians to their comic poets. Bitter satirical comment is combined with scathing political attack, subtle innuendo as well as crude vilification; all of which are used in plays which were produced as part of a competitive religious festival. *Acharnians* written in 425 BC (preceded only by *Banqueters* in 427 BC and *Babylonians* in 426 BC) suggests that the comic writers could not with impunity write as they chose. From references within the play we learn that Aristophanes was prosecuted by Cleon in 426 BC after the production of *Babylonians*, in which he had allegedly 'slandered the city in the presence of foreigners'. It would seem that the charge was dismissed by the council (who decided whether there was a case to answer), for no trial is mentioned. Nevertheless, Aristophanes says that he 'very nearly drowned' (p. 66) and the fact that his comments concerning Cleon in *Acharnians* are guarded suggests that the comic poet was chastened by the experience. Yet this was only until the following year, for in *Knights* of 424 BC Aristophanes launched his most vitriolic attack upon Cleon. The abuse continued as is evident in *Clouds* (p. 137) and *Wasps* (lines 895 ff.) where Cleon is satirized as a dog. And so, it would seem, did the counter charges (cf. *Wasps*, lines 1284-91). Although leading political figures are often fair game for the satirist, Aristophanes must have touched a raw nerve. Indeed, Cleon's reaction (at least as reported by Aristophanes) would seem to imply that what was written was far more than playful jest. The comic poets were, as they liked to think (cf. *Acharnians*, p. 71; *Frogs*, ll. 686 ff.) , dealing didactically with important issues. It could happen, therefore, that they had to face criticism and censure.

The Peloponnesian War broke out in 431 BC, one of the causes being the Megarian Decree. The decree which banned Megarians from the agora of Athens and from the harbours of the empire was made because some Megarians had allegedly cultivated sacred ground. In detailing the reasons for the war Thucydides focuses attention elsewhere, upon incidents which occurred at Potidaea and Epidamnus and upon Spartan fear of Athenian expansion. But at I 139 he says that at one time the Spartans had declared that the war could be avoided if the decree were repealed. The same historian also records that there were some at Athens who felt that the decree should not be maintained at the risk of war. However, Pericles would not yield on this point, interpreting it as a matter of principle. His advice prevailed.

After only a few years of the war Athenian morale was at a low ebb, most especially because of the destruction caused by the annual invasions of the Peloponnesians into Attica, the resultant overcrowding of the country people within the city and the terrible effects of the plague. The frustrations of the people were vented upon their leaders and in particular upon Pericles, who was prosecuted, fined and relieved of his generalship. It may well have been at this later date, when people were in their despair keen to apportion blame, that the Megarian Decree was given a prominence it had not formerly had, and Pericles was said to be responsible for both it and the outbreak of the war. This may well acount for the different emphases given to the reasons for the outbreak of the war by Thucydides and later writers like Aristophanes (cf. *Acharnians*, pp. 71-3; *Peace*, ll. 603-14), Andocides (III 8) and Plutarch (*Pericles*, 29-32). Of course it is possible that, by playing down the significance of the Megarian Decree, Thucydides was protecting Pericles from any blame attached to the issuing of the decree, and that Aristophanes and the others preserve the more accurate picture. Alternatively, Aristophanes may have been misled by the mood of the time, over-emphasizing the role of Pericles and the significance of the decree. No doubt there were those at the outbreak of the war in 431 BC who had argued that the Megarian Decree was not an issue over which peace should be sacrificed, who in 426/5 BC insisted upon the wisdom of their former arguments. It is not easy to know whether Aristophanes wished to impress this point upon his audience in an endeavour to persuade them to consider peace. But whatever the truth may be, Aristophanes' presentation of the Megarian Decree, using as it does both parody of Euripides' *Telephus* and of the first book of Herodotus' history, should remind us that there is also much humour here; and to separate serious comment from burlesque is, as ever in Aristophanes, very difficult. It is noticeable and perhaps significant in this respect that there are different approaches to basically the same issue in two other plays. In *Peace* the events which precipitate the Megarian Decree are different. In both *Peace* and *Lysistrata* the desire for peace is more altruistic. Dikaiopolis makes a private treaty which he jealously guards; he will only give to the bride. *Acharnians* then is not so much a plea for peace as an ordinary man's cry of despair at the pointless-ness of continuing the war and the mismanagement of affairs.

LYSISTRATA

Lysistrata has planned a meeting of the wives whose husbands are fighting in the Peloponnesian War. At the beginning of the play she is waiting for her counterparts from Sparta, Thebes, Corinth and elsewhere, whom she will call upon to refuse sexual intercourse to their husbands until they agree to make peace. When eventually the decision is confirmed by the taking of an oath, each returns to her own country to take up the strike. Lysistrata and her young companions join the older women of Athens who have occupied the Acropolis in order to prevent the use of the state revenues housed there.

The chorus of this play is divided. A group of old men (presumably twelve) appear first, carrying wood and lighted torches to smoke out the women who have blockaded themselves within the Acropolis. A chorus of old women equal in number to the men closely follow, bringing with them pitchers of water to frustrate the men's intentions. The contest between the two groups is won by the women who dowse the men and their torches with their water. A *proboulos*, one of the especially appointed magistrates whose responsibility it was to keep a tight control of affairs after the disastrous campaign in Sicily in 413 BC, has heard of the seizure of the Acropolis by the women and has come with state policemen to put an end to this scandalous behaviour which he blames upon the complacency of husbands and the sexual intemperance of their wives. His men, however, are chased off by the women (a concession to comic licence) and he alone is left to dispute with Lysistrata, arguing that war is the concern of men. Lysistrata contends that war is equally a concern for women, since they suffer the departure of their sons and husbands to war and many of them are left at home unwed, childless and growing old. She argues, using the analogy of spinning, that women have the intelligence (which in antiquity seems to have been much doubted) to run the state effectively. The *proboulos* is mockingly dressed as a woman and given the implements for spinning wool. Finally he is garlanded and treated as a corpse.

We return next, after a considerable delay which heightens anticipation, to the sex strike and its effects. A male is spotted approaching the Acropolis. He is Cinesias the husband of Myrrhine whom he is desperate to meet as his erect condition well illustrates. Myrrhine comes out from the Acropolis but refuses intercourse until Cinesias agrees to make peace. The frustrated male can only think of gratifying his sexual desires. Myrrhine delays, teasing by her repeated fetching of different articles to make their lying together more comfortable. On the point of sexual fulfilment (when no promise of making peace has been extracted but only a concession 'to think about it') Myrrhine disappears back to the Acropolis. Just as one male has been brought to the point of capitulation, soon all will be, for a Spartan herald now enters to tell of the desperate situation in his own country and to plead that steps be taken to resolve this. Noticeably it is the Spartans who first weaken and take the initial steps towards a negotiation of peace. The officials of both states are summoned to a meeting at which Lysistrata presides together with a young and beautiful personification of reconciliation. While the envoys of Sparta and the Athenian magistrates are all eyes for the naked body of Reconciliation, Lysistrata lectures both sides upon their debt to each other because of the mutual help previously given to one another and because of their common heritage. Peace is concluded and the party begins.

After the Athenian defeat in Sicily in 413 BC the Peloponnesians must have been more confident of bringing the war to a successful conclusion. Enormous losses of men and ships had been incurred by the Athenians, and the fortification of Decelea brought even greater pressure to bear upon them, since they were unable to work their land, keep open their land routes to Euboea, and, most importantly, mine silver at Laurion. The Persians too had entered the war, providing money for the procuring of crews to wrest from Athens her Aegean empire. Syracusan aid added to the Spartan naval strength, posing for the first time a real threat to Athenian supremacy in the Aegean. In view of this one might imagine that in 411 BC, the year of the production of *Lysistrata*, the Athenians would be so despondent that the making of peace would be a very real concern. The evidence of *Lysistrata* does not suggest this.

Immediately after Sicily the Athenians began rebuilding their fleet. Ten *probouloi* were appointed with exceptional powers, and the 1000 talents which had been laid aside by Pericles in 431 BC for just such an emergency were used to rebuild and re-equip. Samos was made the centre for naval operations. From here the Athenians successfully campaigned against cities which had been encouraged to revolt by the Spartans (Mytilene, Clazomenai, Chios). The mood of *Lysistrata* does not reflect a desperate despondency nor a panic to make peace at any cost, but a reliance upon Athenian resources and a confidence that Athens could secure favourable terms, if not win the war. For in the play it is the Spartans who are the first to be forced to submit by the women's strike. The final scene with Reconciliation shows them to be outbargained. Furthermore, although finances were tight, the Athenians had no reason to assume that their defeat was imminent, indeed this was another seven years away. It is therefore hard to deny that the play is any less positive in its approach to war than *Acharnians*, written when the Athenians were in a stronger position. The strength or weakness of Athens is insignificant to the argument for peace in the play. Peace, argues Lysistrata, should be sought because of the shared heritage and the former glories of both sides. The enemy should be Persia, as repeated references to the Persian wars make clear, and the grand traditions of the past should be followed. (Presumably it was not then known at Athens that Alcibiades was planning a return to his native city bringing the financial support of Tissaphernes, the Persian Satrap.) The Spartans are Greeks and no different from the Athenians, for as the end of the play emphasizes they are equally eager to sing and dance and enjoy themselves, and they too worship Athena.

> Pray that Athena never
> Her link tae Sparta sever,
> May she protect forever
> Sparta the brave!

To describe *Lysistrata* as a good romp, as if it were no more than that, is inadequate. There is indeed much here to amuse and to excite; the sexual and bibulous profligacy of women, the stock comic reversal of roles, the satirical denigration of those in authority, the virtual staging of the sexual act and a finale with much singing and dancing. But there is also much which informs.

. It might well be contended that if Aristophanes had anything serious to say about peace, bearing in mind the contemporary social status of women, he would have better made his point without Lysistrata and her companions. In fact to pretend that in reality a sex strike and the desperation for intercourse might drive the husbands to make peace, overlooking the possibility of recourse to slaves, prostitutes and concubines, is naive. It is scarcely less fantastical to portray women dictating to men than to imagine a peasant farmer achieving a personal peace as Dikaiopolis in *Acharnians* or the hero riding on a dung-beetle to heaven, as Trygaios in *Peace*. And yet *Lysistrata*, for all the mockery of women's drunkenness and sexual weaknesses, is far more down to earth than either of Aristophanes' previous two peace plays. There is arguably a closer reflection of reality in the depiction and treatment of women and their activities; at home spinning, carrying water, marrying; in religion as attendants and priestesses, and in the women-only festivals of the Thesmophoria and the Skirophoria; in their argumentation for greater social harmony and a return to the normality of domestic life with their husbands at home from war. These aspects and issues raise the play above pure escapism.

Indeed, Lysistrata is a sympathetic figure who is authoritative in her organisation of her women followers, convincing in her rebuttal of the *proboulos* and victorious in her bringing of reconciliation at the end of the play. Since she is sympathetic, so, it is reasonable to assume, is her cause. But care is needed here, for the cause of peace which is argued throughout the play is voiced by comic characters who, although the creations of Aristophanes, do not necessarily speak for him. They speak in comic and utopian terms, and, although the issues of war and peace are serious ones, they are presented in a manner appropriate to the identity of the speaker (and not the author) and through a medium associated with a competitive festival (and not an assembly or law court). No practical details of the Athenian situation post-Sicily nor of the significance of the Persian interference nor yet of the many obstacles to peace are confronted, but we are presented with a deliberately uncontentious and idealistic belief that all Greeks share a common heritage which should be honoured and celebrated. To this all may nod their assent, but few would seriously entertain such proposals for peace knowing that real life is scarcely this simple. Great caution is therefore needed in any attempt to detect the views of Aristophanes, despite the fact that he makes the theme of peace central to three of his plays.

Clouds

p. 112 Aristophanes has three different ways of beginning a play: (1) a monologue (as here and in *Acharnians*) which explains the situation to the audience; (2) a lively dialogue which arouses our curiosity and is then broken off (as in *Wasps* and *Peace*) by one of the characters, who turns to address us; and (3) a dialogue (as in *Frogs*) from which we have to piece the situation together.

I heard the cock ages ago: Water-clocks were used in Athenian lawcourts, but we do not hear of clocks of any kind in domestic use. People judged the time during the day by the sun, and the approach of dawn by cockcrow.

They'd never have dared to: Complaints about lazy and stupid slaves are a cliché of comedy, but here there is a special point in the complaint. Athens had been at war since 431; in each of the first six years of the war an enemy force had invaded Attica, and Boeotia, which bordered Attica on the north, was one of Athens' enemies. Slaves belonging to cruel Athenian masters therefore had opportunities to desert, and there was no way of getting them back.

Bitten all over: As if by vermin.

He grows his hair long: This was characteristic of young men of wealthy and distinguished families.

In his chariot and pair: Chariots were used in Classical times only for racing, not for war.

The twenty-fourth or twenty-fifth of the month: Interest on a debt became payable at the end of the month.

Boy!: The word *pais* was used for 'son', 'daughter', 'boy', 'girl', 'child' and 'slave' (of any age).

p. 113 **A number of waxed tablets**: Papyrus was used for books, but temporary records were scratched into a coating of wax on a wooden tablet; when no longer needed, the record was erased by warming up the wax. The tablets were commonly hinged together like a loose-leaf folder.

One thousand two hundred drachmas: A drachma was a day's pay for a skilled man at this time.

The horse with the Q brand: There is nothing about the branding of horses in Xenophon's *Horsemanship*, but some Attic vases show horses with brand-marks on their hindquarters.

A bailiff, I think: Literally, 'a demarch' – the elected official of the 'deme' (a unit of locality, like 'village' in the country or 'quarter' in the town), who kept a register of the property-qualifications of all the members of the deme and had the authority to enforce the surrender of securities for debt.

p. 114   **The matchmaker**: In middle- and upper-class Athenian society the sexes were segregated, and it was not easy for a young man and a girl to meet and talk. In such a society there is a role for the old woman who acts as a go-between and can urge a man to make an approach to a girl's father and ask for her in marriage.

The niece of Megacles: The Greek text has 'niece of Megacles son of Megacles' and there actually was such a man alive at the time, and a wealthy man at that. He did not necessarily have a real niece, and Aristophanes may have picked on the name simply because it recurred in one great family (the Alcmaeonidae, to whom Pericles belonged on his mother's side); it also suggests 'great renown' (*mega kleos*).

A right Coesyra: A lady of aristocratic family who 'put on airs', two or three generations earlier.

Saffron: Used as a dye for expensive dresses.

Remind him of those damn horses: 'Horse' is *hippos*. The element *-(h)ippus* or *-(h)ippides* is common in names and certainly not peculiar to the upper classes, but 'Xanthippus' was a famous name – Pericles' father, in fact.

Pheidonides: The stem *pheid-* means 'save (money etc.)', 'parsimonious'.

After his grandad: This was a very common Greek practice.

Pheidippides: The name itself is not intrinsically comic, because 'Pheidippus' is common, and we know of more than one Pheidippides well before Aristophanes' time, but in this context the combination of 'horse' with 'parsimonious' is a joke.

Ride in procession: As we see in the Parthenon frieze, which depicts the procession at the festival Panathenaea.

p. 115   **Kiss me and put your right hand in mine**: The kiss of kinship and friendship was exchanged between men, as in most cultures (in *Frogs*, l. 788 we are told that the ghost of Sophocles kissed the ghost of Aeschylus when they met in the underworld), and clasping right hands was not only a greeting but a solemn pledge of goodwill.

By Poseidon the god of horses: Poseidon was also the god of the sea and of earthquakes (cf. p. 136).

The house next door: Literally, 'Do you see that little house and little door?', where the diminitive suffixes implying 'little' should probably not be taken too literally; Strepsiades is cajoling his son, implying 'Now, there's nothing to be scared of' and 'I'm not really asking you for very much'. He is obviously pointing to a door in the stage-building, and the restive modern reader, who has accepted that the scene so far has been enacted in a bedroom inside a house, begins to wonder where we are now. The answer is that we are now required to forget entirely about the bedroom (at some point the beds must be removed, but the text does not reveal exactly when or how). See also note on 'I'm only a countryman', p. 117.

p. 116   **Like one of those round things**: Bread was baked in a dome-shaped oven heated by fuel beneath and around it. The theory that the universe is of that shape was put forward by a certain Hippon, about whom we know nothing else; but it was not an ephemeral idea, since it recurs (attributed to the astronomer Meton) in *Birds*, ll. 1000 f.

Philosophers: *Merimnophrontistai*, a made-up word analysable as 'thinkers about difficult problems'.

White-faced barefoot characters: 'White-faced' because they do not spend their time in healthy outdoor sports or in honest work on the land. 'Barefoot' because Socrates habitually went barefoot. Intellectuals were regarded as indifferent to the pleasures and comforts of life, and as impoverished because they did no profitable work. Yet at the same time they were regarded as delicate in health and pampered by wealthy patrons. This contradiction runs all through the play.

Chaerephon: Several passages in the first part of the play give us the impression that Chaerephon is going to be an important character in it, but he never appears except perhaps (very briefly) in the last scene. In Plato's *Apology* 20E Socrates calls him 'a friend of mine ever since we were young'. A passage in *Wasps* (ll. 1412 f.) suggests that he was pale and thin.

All the pheasants in Athens: Pheasants, like peacocks, were imported from the East as exotic birds for display, but were not bred for food.

They have two Arguments in there – Right and Wrong: Later on (pp. 149 ff.) we shall see Right and Wrong arguing against each other, and that accounts for what may seem to us the odd notion 'they *have*

two Arguments *in* there'. See also note on 'Which of the arguments
do you want?', p. 167.

Needn't pay anyone an obol: An obol was one sixth of a drachma.
It is often treated (as here) as if it were the smallest of all coins, but
in fact there were eight *khalkoi* to an obol.

p. 117   **But...not out of the house**: He actually says, 'I'll go indoors'; see
the note on 'the house next door' (p. 115).

Boy! My little boykins!: Anyone knocking at the door of an
Athenian house assumes that it will be opened by a slave; see the note
on 'Boy!' (p. 112). But Socrates' school seems to have no slaves; the
man who opens the door to Strepsiades behaves towards the other
students (p. 120) as a person in authority.

Strepsiades is my name: The stem *strep-* means 'turn', 'twist'.
Worry about his debts made the old man 'toss and turn' at night (p.
113). He wants to learn how to 'twist and turn' to escape his creditors
(p. 131); 'twister' is (in the Greek text) one of the unfriendly names to
which 'let men call me names' refers on that same page; and at the
end of the play 'by making love to evil crookery' (p. 171) is literally
'twisting yourself into bad doings'. All the same, 'Strepsiades' is not a
made-up name; one of Pindar's victory-odes (*Isthmian* 7) is addressed
to a Theban Strepsiades, forty years before this play.

From Cicynna: See note on demes (p. 113). Cicynna was an obscure name, perhaps a stock joke among city-dwellers.

I'm only a countryman: Literally, 'I live far off in the country'. For
the purpose of this passage, we have to think of Strepsiades' house
and Socrates' school as miles apart; for the purpose of other passages
(pp. 115 f., 172) we have to imagine they are close together.

It is not lawful to divulge it: There were many 'mystery-religions'
in the Greek world, into which people could be initiated, and no-one
was allowed to divulge to others the secrets revealed to him in his
initiation. Admission to the school of Socrates is treated as a kind of
initiation into mysteries (cf. pp. 122 f.). Plato himself on occasion
spoke in similar terms of progress in philosophy (*Symposium* 209E is
a notable example), but his Socrates does not require ritual pro-
cedures or attempt to confine philosophy to a closed community of
initiates.

p. 118   **He used a most elegant method**: We hear little about scientific
experiments in the Classical period, and we gain the impression that
Greek scientists preferred abstract speculation. This passage implies
that our impression may be misleading.

Pair of slippers: Fleas have six feet, but we think of slippers in pairs – and do not, as a rule, think of entomology while watching a comedy.

Groans under the force of the wind: Speculative scientists (particularly Alcmaeon) had written of the sound-effects of forcing air through a narrow passage into a chamber, but the playing of wind-instruments will have acquainted people with the principle anyway.

p. 119 **He sprinkled a little ash on the table**: Papyrus was too expensive to be used for mathematical exercises, so the Greeks drew with a point in ash, dust or sand.

He whipped somebody's coat: With the compasses, presumably; and sold the coat to buy food. Stealing clothes was one of the 'standard' crimes at Athens. The odd thing is that the Greek text says not 'somebody's coat' but 'the coat', and that is not easily explained. Possibly 'he got his coat' (i.e. the coat he's wearing, for which Greek would say 'the' rather than 'his') 'by stealing it from the wrestling-school' was a derogatory remark commonly made of a down-and-out.

Thales: A famous speculative thinker of the early sixth century, from Miletus. He was the subject of anecdotes and the prototype of the 'absent-minded professor'.

Spartan prisoners from Pylos: In 425 a Spartan force on the island of Sphacteria, beside Pylos in the south-west Peloponnese, was cut off by Athenian ships and forced to surrender. The prisoners were brought to Athens and held there as hostages to preclude any further Peloponnesian invasion of Attica. The Spartans had hitherto been regarded as invincible on land, and it gave the Athenians great pleasure to see their prisioners humiliated and deteriorating physically.

p. 120 **The lowest reaches of hell**: Literally 'what is below the earth', which does not have the frightening associations of our word 'hell', though it includes the world of the dead.

Go inside: Since the students were revealed by the opening of the door (p. 119) we have been thinking of them as 'inside' already. In the theatre, either they were revealed by the moving of a screen or they were pushed out of the stage-building as a tableau on a trolley. In either case, they now have to enter the stage-building and leave behind them the instruments with which the next passage of dialogue is concerned.

In a new settlement: *Geometria* is literally 'measurement of land', and Strepsiades thinks at once of occasions on which the Athenians confiscated land from a rebellious subject-ally and allocated it to Athenian citizens. That is 'democratic' in the sense that ordinary citizens profit from it.

A map of the whole world: Probably a very schematic diagram on a board; the idea of maps was slow to gain ground in the ancient world.

Where are the jurymen?: It is a standard joke in comedy that the Athenians are litigious and love to spend their time sitting on juries.

p. 121　**The island of Euboea**: Euboea, about 110 miles long, runs northwest to south-east off the coasts of Boeotia and Attica.

Me and Pericles: The cities of Euboea were subject-allies of Athens. In 445 they rebelled, and the rebellion was decisively suppressed by an Athenian force under Pericles' command. It is worthwhile to remind ourselves from time to time that Aristophanes' audience was largely composed of men with repeated experience of hand-to-hand fighting; and the same is true of his male characters (including Socrates, Euripides, etc.).

Swings into view: Suspended from the top of a crane, the *mekhane* (our word 'machine'), which was used to represent characters flying through the air.

Why call'st me, O thou creature of a day?: For comic effect Aristophanes often makes a character speak high-flown poetic language – either an actual quotation or simply a parody of the style – and Socrates here speaks as if he were a deity looking down upon an earthbound mortal.

The Mysteries of the gods: Although Anaxagoras had argued that the sun is a lump of red-hot material, it was a god in popular belief; cf. 'the sun declared...', p. 137.

p. 122　**Of very similar constitution to thought**: The passage parodies the doctrine of Diogenes of Apollonia: that the human soul is a form of air; that perception is the movement of air in the body caused by air without; and that thinking is an activity of soul-air, impaired by the nearness of earth and moisture. We do not know how (if at all) Diogenes used the analogy of watercress, but a plant that draws up a great deal of moisture is a pretty obvious analogy.

To be made an orator: Literally, 'to learn to speak'. Since people were often prosecuted by adversaries for political acts, and since victory and defeat in non-political cases affected political status, the Athenians tended not to differentiate between skill in addressing juries and skill in addressing political assemblies.

Ah, but what gods?: The correct translation is 'What do you mean, "swear by gods"?'

No longer current: Literally, 'not current coin' (*nomisma*, 'currency', 'legal tender').

What is the currency you swear by?: Literally, 'with what' (not 'by what') 'do you swear?', i.e. 'What do you use for oaths?'

Like they have at Byzantium: The Greek city which stood in Classical times where Constantinople stood later was of some military importance because of its position on the straits, but not particularly large or powerful. It seems that it was unusual in using iron for coins of low denomination.

On the sacred bed: Presumably one of the objects left behind when the students went 'indoors'. Socrates is performing a ritual of initiation on Strepsiades: (1) 'enthronement', (2) crowning him with a garland, and (3) sprinkling him with flour, a kind of 'baptism'.

p. 123   **Like Athamas in the play**: Both Sophocles and Xenocles made tragedies out of the myth of Athamas. Commanded by an oracle to sacrifice his children, he was compelled, when they had escaped him, to offer himself as a sacrifice instead. Garlands were put on the heads of victims, and on their sacrificers. The fact that Athamas' wife was Nephele ('Cloud') gives an added appropriateness to the reference.

Flowery speaker and floury already: *Paipale*, 'fine flour', is a metaphor for 'subtle speaker' in a derogatory sense.

Keep silence all: The usual formula at the utterance of any public prayer or invocation. In this case there is an audience of one.

On whom the earth supported floats: Diogenes of Apollonia again; but also Anaxagoras and others before him.

And Ether bright: The Greeks distinguished between *aer*, the air close to the earth (sometimes 'mist', 'fog'), and *aither*, the upper air.

Come, holy Clouds: Socrates' invocation follows a traditional pattern, calling on the Clouds to hear the prayer 'wherever you are, whether in...or in...or in...', to accept the offering (but Socrates does not seem to be making them any offering), and to *come* to the worshipper; Greek prayer assumes that a god will *hear* from any distance but does not expect him to *act* at a distance.

Your father Ocean's bower: The Greeks thought that Ocean encircled the whole earth.

Mimas' peak: Mimas is a mountain on the Aegean coast of Asia Minor.

p. 124   **Scythia bleak**: From the lower Danube round the northern half of the Black Sea to north of the Caucasus.

Singing in the distance: It is clear from the dialogue which follows that we do not see the Chorus until after they have sung their two stanzas. This is a producer's nightmare in a modern theatre, for it is extremely hard to hear the words of what is being sung offstage, and it is not easy even in an open-air Greek theatre. It is possible, however, if Socrates and Strepsiades have moved towards the front of the orchestra and Socrates is gazing northwards, that the chorus has already entered the back of the orchestra and is in full view of the audience; then, when Socrates says 'coming in by the side' (p. 125), he swings round, Strepsiades does the same, and the joke is thereby heightened.

CHORUS: In the first stanza the Clouds exhort one another to move from Ocean to the earth ('the world to view' in the fourth verse and 'to earth direct your gaze' in the last). In the second stanza they are more specific; they are coming to Athens ('where Athena rules the loveliest land in Greece').

I fain would blow a fart: Deadly fear can have a disturbing effect on the bowels (a fact better known to the battle-hardened Greeks than to most of us), and Aristophanic comedy translates emotion into physiological terms whenever possible.

Nor do as those comedians base: Comedy can sometimes raise a laugh by reference to its own character.

p. 125   **The glorious Mysteries**: The Eleusinian Mysteries were the most famous in the Greek world, and the Athenians took great pride in the fact that people came from far and wide to be initiated at a sanctuary which belonged to Athens.

Lofty, beauteous temples: Athens was by no means unique in the size and number of its temples, but the situation of the Acropolis – in the centre of the city, and high, but not too high – gave the Parthenon, the Propylaea and other buildings on the Acropolis an extraordinary beauty and impressiveness.

Festival and sacrifice: Thucydides makes Pericles in the Funeral Speech (Thuc. II 38.1) boast of the number and scale of festivals and sacrifices at Athens. A Greek sacrifice was an occasion not for self-abasement but for feasting and display.

Dionysus: The City Dionysia, held in the spring, was a great festival which included the performance of tragedies and comedies; this play was performed on that occasion in 423, so that reference to the festival is the right note on which to end the Chorus' song.

Ancestral heroines: Many of the great figures of myth were thought of as 'half-gods', of mixed divine and human parentage; Helen, for example, was a daughter of Zeus by a mortal woman. They, and other outstanding figures associated with them in myth, were called 'heroes' and 'heroines', endowed with supernatural powers and made the object of prayer, sacrifice and invocation in local cults.

The layabout: See the more detailed note on p. 126.

Towards Mount Parnes: Parnes is the range which extends most of the way across the northern border of Attica. Clouds do indeed gather there; but the humorous point in this passage is that from the theatre Parnes is completely hidden by the Acropolis.

Coming in by the side: Comedy, unlike tragedy, sometimes breaks dramatic illusion by explicit reference to the theatre or to the audience.

p. 126 **Sophists**: In the fifth century *sophistes* was used of someone who practised and taught any art or skill (including poetry, music, pottery and divination) or pursued any branch of specialised knowledge. At the time of this play it had begun to be applied especially to those who taught verbal skills; by the next generation it had become a derogatory term.

Prophets: Prophecy was founded almost entirely on the interpretation of omens and of oracles transmitted in written collections, very rarely on individual inspiration.

Teachers of medicine: Some writers on medicine sought to explain sickness and health on highly theoretical general principles, attaching much importance to climate, so that clouds are relevant to medicine.

Dithyrambs: The dithyramb was a genre of choral lyric performed at festivals of Dionysus. Comic poets, thinking of themselves as 'down-to-earth', ridicule dithyrambic poets for their elaborate, high-flown language.

Typhon: A mythical giant beneath the earth, generator of violent storms.

Thrushes' avian flesh: Strepsiades deliberately speaks 'poetic' language. Payment for the production of choral performances was a form of taxation imposed on the rich, and naturally the poet would be invited to the banquet given by the producer after the performance.

p. 127 **Centaurs**: Centaurs were imaginary creatures which had the torsos, arms and heads of men joined to the bodies and legs of horses (and how many lungs, livers, etc., we are never told). Except for the wise and virtuous centaur Chiron, they were wild creatures, given to drunken violence and rape.

Hairy sex-maniacs: A strong growth of hair on head or body was popularly regarded as a sign of great sexual appetite.

Xenophantus' son: A man called Hieronymus.

Simon: We do not know whether he did 'rifle public funds' – or, if so, when and how. We are very often in that position with people ridiculed in comedy.

Deer: Proverbially timid.

Cleonymus: A regular butt of the comic poets for alleged cowardice.

Cleisthenes: This man seems to have had difficulty in growing a full beard (the Athenians did not shave), and he is ridiculed in comedy as effeminate.

p. 128   **Only Prodicus**: One of the most distinguished of the intellectuals who visited Athens in the late fifth century and enjoyed the patronage of rich families. He interested himself in language, prescribing rules of usage and offering definitions; he was also the author of a moralising myth, *The Choice of Herakles*, which upheld traditional values.

And cuss: The text actually says 'glancing sideways', which suggests alertness rather than 'cussing'.

Who sends the rain: Zeus had many of the characteristics of a weather-god and sky-god and was invoked when rain was needed.

Necessarily: Where we speak of 'laws' of nature, the Greeks spoke of 'necessity'.

It's a whirl in the sky: Democritus, a contemporary of Aristophanes, postulated a whirling motion which at the beginning of time had sorted the universe out into its constituent elements.

p. 129   **Zeus is dead**: It was widely believed that in remote times Uranus was overthrown by his son Cronus and Cronus in turn overthrown by his own son Zeus, so that the idea of a succession of rulers in heaven is not alien to Strepsiades.

The Pan-Athenian Festival: This was held about a month after midsummer and, like most festivals, was an occasion for over-eating and heavy drinking.

Phartos: The text says 'that's why *bronte* (thunder) and *porde* (fart) are alike'.

People who perjure themselves: In Greek society documentation was negligible and the techniques of detecting criminals rudimentary; hence much turned on witnesses and on the swearing of oaths. Perjury was therefore a form of wrongdoing which was felt more than anything else to undermine law and order, and since it involved the gods directly (cf. the note on 'in a place of my choice', p. 162), the perjurer was believed to incur divine punishment in this world and the next.

Methuselah?: On several occasions in the play (cf. p. 150) exponents of the 'new thinking' decry their opponents as 'antediluvian', 'prehistoric', and the like. The rate of change in fifth-century Greek society was very slow indeed compared to what we are experiencing, but fast enough to make it possible to use 'old-fashioned' and equivalent terms in a derogatory sense.

Simon, Cleonymus and Theorus: Cf. the note on Simon, p. 127.

Why?: The traditional believer could well answer, 'Because the gods are not always quick to punish. Wait and see'.

His own temple...at Sunium: A decisive argument against the idea that lightning is solely a weapon against perjurers; but no argument at all against the belief that the punishment of perjurers is *one* of its purposes.

p. 130   **His own oak trees**: The oak was especially associated with Zeus.

When a dry wind in the sky gets shut up: The theory that thunder and lightning are caused by wind bursting out of dense cloud goes back to the sixth century; nearer to Aristophanes' time, the friction of clouds had been postulated as the cause of lightning, and their collision as the cause of thunder.

If you laugh at the cold: Endurance of cold and hunger and resistance to the temptations of pleasure and comfort were admired and regarded as characteristic of the good citizen-soldier; here there is an implication (by including 'wrestling') that such resistance also distinguishes the intellectual from normal, reasonable men.

Only the gods that we believe in: Earlier (p. 123) Socrates invoked Air and Ether, and later (p. 138) he will swear by Respiration and Air; but comedy does not trouble too much about consistency in small matters. 'Chaos' here does not mean 'confusion', but the Empty Space which (in traditional myth as well as scientific speculation) was the first thing to exist.

p. 131   **Carries more resolutions**: See the note on 'to be made an orator', p. 122.

CHORUS: **If he has them for his dinner**: The repetitions here and on p. 132, in the manner of Gilbert and Sullivan, are not in the Greek text; cf. p. 37 of the translation.

p. 132   **To consult you**: The Athenians had no professional 'barristers' or 'solicitors'. A man who was skilful in litigation and forensic speaking would advise a friend, then a friend's friend, and so on; and if successful, he would become widely known as an unofficial 'consultant' and speech-writer. Naturally his 'clients' would show their gratitude to him in material ways (hence 'will make you really wealthy' below), but it would have been thought shameless, and therefore disadvantageous to them, if they had openly revealed in court that they had paid money to someone for putting their case together.

p. 133   **I wait a little**: The point of raising a cry is to secure witnesses to the assault itself; by 'waiting a little' one could try to claim falsely to have been the victim of assault.

Plant something here: A man who believed that another man had stolen something from him was allowed to go in and search that man's house, in the presence of the demarch (see note on 'a bailiff', p. 113), but had to strip before doing so.

p. 134   **I might as well be dead**: Chaerephon is ridiculed in comedy for his pallor.

A honey-cake to feed the snakes with: In Boeotia there was a cave dedicated to the hero Trophonius, into which people went to receive oracular responses. They made offerings of honey-cakes to placate the snakes which lived, or were believed to live, in the cave.

CHORUS: Here begins the 'parabasis', the portion of the comedy in which the actors are all offstage and the chorus addresses the audience directly. After the first address, 'I swear by Dionysus...' down to 'a generation wise' (p. 136) come two choral songs, each of which is followed by a further address to the audience. The two songs are commonly, as here, invocations to gods. Though it suspends its role in relation to the personages of the play and the fictitious situation portrayed therein, the chorus retains its own character; from 'Zeus, thou almighty...' (p. 136) down to the end of the parabasis ('to count your days', p. 138) the chorus speaks as if it were a company of clouds which has come to Athens to sing and dance for us on the occasion of the City Dionysia. The first address, however, has a very unusual feature. Instead of making the chorus praise his merits as a comic poet and denigrate his rivals – as Aristophanes does in his other plays of the 420s – he treats the chorus-leader simply as a mouthpiece, so that 'I' means 'I, Aristophanes, the poet'. Since the passage refers to the failure of *Clouds* in 423 and to plays produced by other poets in and after 421, it must have been composed for the revised version of the play.

My protector in my youth: Success and achievement were attributed to the help and favour of gods, though the mechanisms by which they gave this help were uncertain. A man who discovered in himself a talent for writing comedies would be inclined to say that he was 'brought up' or 'protected' by Dionysus.

So may I lose: The idiom 'So may X happen, if Y is not the case' is a way of asserting Y strongly.

First be tasted by this city: It is highly doubtful whether an Athenian comic poet could have put on a play anywhere else.

p. 135   **The Banqueters I mean**: See the end of Section I of the Introduction.

Like an unwed mother: The abandonment of illegitimate babies was normal. Since the mortality rate of legitimate children was high, a good many abandoned babies may have been picked up by people who wanted them. Aristophanes is referring here to the fact that he was not himself the producer of his earliest plays.

As I submit: But it is an impudent submission; admiration for a writer's first work does not commit us to indiscriminate admiration of everything he writes thereafter.

Like Electra...her brother's hair: Electra, daughter of Agamemnon, longed for her brother Orestes to come home from exile and avenge their father by killing their mother and her lover. When Orestes came and left a lock of his hair as an offering on Agamemnon's tomb, Electra found the hair and recognised it as his. She did not, in any version of the myth known to us, go 'looking here and there', but stayed at home waiting, and Orestes' return took her by surprise. Aristophanes' recollection of the story is as hazy as his recollection of Aeschylus' *Persians* in *Frogs*, ll. 102 f.

Great thick...tool: It is very unlikely that Aristophanes discarded the 'phallus' (artificial penis) which was a traditional feature of comic costume. He probably means that other playwrights made great play with outsize phalli; and since the Greeks never practised circumcision, 'red-tipped' probably refers to humorous representation of circumcised slaves from Egypt and Phoenicia or (as sometimes in humorous vase-painting) men with inadequate foreskins.

Men who're bald: As Aristophanes himself was (*Peace*, ll. 771 ff.).

A cordax: An uninhibited dance associated with comedy and drunken parties.

A well-aimed poke: As in third-rate farce in all ages, noise and assault could always be used to compensate for lack of wit.

No torches, shouts or violence: Yet *Clouds* itself ends with all those things. We must never treat Aristophanes' boasting and denigration of his rivals as if he were a scrupulous historian of literature. Similarly he claims below 'I always think up new ideas...' at the very moment when he is re-hashing *Clouds* with the intention – and he presumably did have such an intention, even though he abandoned it in the end – of putting it on again.

Not a long-haired fop: Cf. above, on his baldness, 'long-haired weirdies' on p. 126 and note on 'wears his hair long', p. 112.

I always think up new ideas: Aristophanes criticises novelty and modernity in serious poetry and music, but boasts of originality in his own art.

p. 136   **I went for Cleon**: *Knights*, produced in 424, is a sustained and virulent attack on Cleon, who between the death of Pericles in 429 and his own death in 422 was the dominant figure on Athenian public life.

But only once: There are however some venomous references to Cleon in *Peace*, produced after Cleon's death.

Hyperbolus: After Cleon's death, a prominent man in politics; 'ostracised' (i.e. exiled for ten years, without confiscation of property) in 416, and murdered in Samos in 411.

And his mother's: It was not customary in the Greek world to spare the mother, wife or children of anyone whom one wished to vilify. Hyperbolus' mother, however, is attacked in her own right in *Thesmophoriazusae*, ll. 839 ff. as a moneylender.

Eupolis, the stinking thief: Eupolis was Aristophanes' most distinguished rival in comedy, and almost equally esteemed for a long time afterwards.

Maricas: Thanks to some papyrus fragments of a commentary on *Maricas*, we know a little about it – but nothing to justify the charge that it was '*Knights* rehashed'. It was produced in 421; and since Aristophanes goes on to say that 'Hermippus then and all the rest' continued to attack Hyperbolus, the passage is further evidence that this section of the parabasis belongs to the revised version of *Clouds*.

Phrynichus: A slightly older contemporary of Aristophanes.

A drunk old woman gobbled by a whale: This sounds like a burlesque version of the myth of Andromeda, who was put on the shore to be devoured by a sea-monster but was rescued by Perseus. The 'drunk old woman' was perhaps identifiable as Hyperbolus' mother.

Hermippus then and all the rest: Hermippus too was a slightly older contemporary of Aristophanes; and the comic poet Plato, who wrote a *Hyperbolus*, is one of 'all the rest'.

My joke about the eels: Presumably a reference to a short passage of *Knights* (ll. 864 ff.), where Aristophanes compares Cleon to an eel-hunter stirring up the mud.

CHORUS: It is traditional in prayers and invocations (cf. the opening of Socrates' invocation on p. 123) to name a series of deities, each described in terms of his or her virtues, activities or favoured places. In most cases the description precedes the name (in the Greek text the song begins, literally, 'high-ruling of gods Zeus king'), or the name may not be used at all: the 'Lord of the Earthquake' is Poseidon, 'him who drives' is the Sun, and (in the second song) 'blest Maid' is

Artemis. The last line of the second song leads to Dionysus as the 'punch-word', literally, 'and Parnassian he who holding rock with pine-torches shines to maenads of Delphi appearing reveller Dionysus'. This is the kind of structural phenomenon, appreciated by the ancient Greek listener, which it is extraordinarily hard to reproduce in translating from verse in one language into verse in another.

Trident: Poseidon was conceived as using his trident to lever up the ground or the sea-bed, causing earthquakes and tidal waves.

p. 137 **Omens bad**: Thunder and rain were taken as signs of divine disapproval.

The Paphlagonian trafficker in leather: Cleon, whatever other sources of income he had (and he was not a parvenu; his father had once been elected a general), seems to have owned a tannery, and Aristophanes exploits that to the full. In *Knights* the 'Paphlagonian slave' of Demos (personification of the People) represents Cleon. It was standard form to allege that an adversary was of non-Greek origin. Aristophanes may have made Cleon a Paphlagonian (Paphlagonia is a region of the Black Sea coast of Asia Minor) because of the word's resemblance to *paphlazein*, 'seethe', 'bubble', 'bluster'.

The moon forsook her path: There was an eclipse of the moon on 29 October 425, and of the sun on 21 March 424. The election of the generals for 424/3 took place early in 424, and Cleon was elected one of them.

Oh yes, you do: But Cleon was killed in battle in 422; this passage, therefore, must come from the original *Clouds*, not from the revision.

Dump him in the stocks: Literally, 'squeeze his neck in the wood', a board with holes for head, hands and feet.

Despite your first false move: Threats and reproaches directed against the audience in a comic parabasis sometimes end on a note of reassurance and encouragement, or with a joke that takes the sting out of the reproaches.

Cynthus' rocky summit: The hill on Delos, the little island in mid-Aegean sacred to Apollo ('Phoebus').

In the Ephesians' temple of gold: There was a famous sanctuary of Artemis ('blest Maid') at Ephesus on the coast of Asia Minor; the Lydians, a non-Greek people who lived inland from Ephesus, took part in her worship.

Our Protectress: Pallas Athena; in saying 'our' the Chorus is speaking as Athenians, not as clouds.

Wielder of the aegis: The 'aegis' of Athena was a short but voluminous cape.

The reveller of Parnassus: Parnassus is the great mountain behind Delphi; for the three midwinter months Apollo, the god of Delphi, was 'out of residence', and Dionysus was worshipped there. The choice of the title 'reveller' (*komastes*) is particularly appropriate in this passage, since *komoidia*, 'comedy', meant 'singing in a procession of revelry'. Just as the second of the pair of stanzas sung by the Chorus on its approach (p. 125) ended with the festival of Dionysus, so Dionysus is the climax of the series of deities invoked in this pair of stanzas.

p. 138   **You've turned the calendar all topsy-turvy**: Greek months were alternately of 29 and 30 days, so that a sequence of 12 lunar months differed by eleven days from a solar year. To reconcile the two, an extra month was intercalated every three years or so. But in addition, odd days were sometimes intercalated (for a variety of reasons), and we know from the texts of treaties given by Thucydides (IV 118.12, 119.1; V 19.1) that the Athenian month was running two days ahead of the Spartan in 423 but two days behind in 421. Festivals were fixed by dates in the lunar calendar; hence the Clouds' complaint that the gods could never be sure when the Athenians would be holding a festival.

From meals are turned away: The prayers and invocations which formed part of a festival asked the gods to be present, to accept the sacrifices and to enjoy the festivities as honoured guests of the human community.

It's her they blame: Rather unreasonably, but she is the nearest to hand.

In mourning fast: Certain festivals included a fast-day in ritual mourning for the death of a hero.

Hyperbolus: See note on p. 136.

His wreath away we blew: We know nothing else of this incident, which was no doubt treated as a disturbing omen.

What with all the bugs: That the bed should be full of bugs is part of the picture of intellectuals as poor and squalid.

p. 139   **Rhythms? Verse measures?**: English (like German and Modern Greek, but unlike French) has a 'stress' accent – i.e. we make more noise on one syllable of a word than on the others – and an English verse-form is a pattern of stresses. Ancient Greek verse-forms were patterns of 'long' and 'short' syllables (e.g. the name *Sokrates*, 'Socrates' is long-short-long, symbolised – ∪ –). The two main types of rhythm are 'double-short' (– ∪∪ – ∪∪ – ∪∪ – ∪∪ ...) and 'single-short' (– ∨ – ∪ – ∪ – ∪ ...). Any given rhythm is used in units of varying sizes (*metra*, 'measures').

Iambic trimeters? Trochaic tetrameters?: The minimal unit of rhythm is ✗ — ᴗ — (where ✗ signifies a position which can be occupied by either a long or a short syllable), and an iambic trimeter is composed of three of those units. The minimal unit of trochaic rhythm is — ᴗ — ✗ , and a tetrameter is four of them, the last being abbreviated to — ᴗ — .

What an anapaest is and a dactyl: These are double-short rhythms; the minimal unit of anapaestic rhythm is ᴗᴗ — ᴗᴗ—, and of dactylic rhythm — ᴗᴗ .

All the other kinds of feet: The term 'foot' was often used of a sequence of two or three syllables. The translation of this passage is (justifiably) very free; the Greek text exploits the anbiguity of *daktulos*, 'dactyl' or 'finger', which cannot be directly reproduced in English.

p. 140 **Which animals are male?**: Protagoras had argued that gram- mar and reality parted company in the gender-classification of some nouns, and he may have argued – as Socrates is just about to do – that linguistic usage should be 'rationalised'.

A chicken: When we say 'chicken' we usually think of a hen, but the Greeks (who enjoyed cock-fighting) would as readily think of a cockerel when they heard the word *alektruon*, which means a domestic fowl of either sex.

'Chickeness' and...'chicker': *Alektruaina* and *alektor* in Greek – both of them invented for the occasion.

For such a feminine object: *Kardopos*, 'kneading- trough', is fem- inine, unlike most nouns ending in *-os*.

That foxy fellow: Introduced into the translation to prepare the way for the humorous analogy between 'trough'/'triffen' and 'fox'/ 'vixen'.

He does his kneading with a round mortar: Probably meant to suggest that Cleonymus (see note on p. 127) masturbates because he has no success with women.

Triffen – vixen – Cleonyme: Socrates suggests that *kardopos* should be replaced by *kardope* (*-e* is a very characteristic ending of feminine nouns), and Strepsiades caps this by turning the name of the effeminate Cleonymus into Cleonyme.

p. 141 **'Hullo, Sandie!'**: The Greek has 'Ameinias', not 'Alexander'. The point of the joke is that a masculine name in - *as* ends in *-a* in the vocative case, and that makes it just like the many feminine names in *-a* (e.g. Demetria).

The way she manages: We know nothing about this Ameinias.

And have some thoughts: Socrates now adopts a 'tutorial method' which is 'unstructured' in the sense that it is entirely up to Strepsiades to allow ideas to come into his head. This is unlike anything to be found in the portrayal of Socrates by Plato and Xenophon, and unlike the magisterial lecturing technique which Plato attributes to the sophists. It reminds us of the 'free association' encouraged by a psychotherapist in a patient; how far it is modelled on any teaching technique actually used in the Greek world, we do not know.

p. 142 **What ails thee, friend?**: The Chorus uses poetic language, as again below in 'Nay, bear it not...', for humorous contrast with Strepsiades' crude lament.

A vast Phlee-asian host: The Phliasians were the people of Phlius, a small city in the north-east Peloponnese. The Greek has 'Corinthians', a pun on *koreis*, 'bugs'.

Uncertain if I'm still a man: Literally (and in the preceding stanza, not this one), 'They're pulling out my balls'.

p. 143 **My prick in my hand**: With 'a juicy something else' (p. 142) Strepsiades' imagination has strayed away from the problem of debts.

A Thessalian slave, a witch: Plato refers (*Gorgias* 513A) to 'Thessalian women who draw the moon down'. We do not know what their clients thought was happening.

p. 144 **It's reckoned by the month**: The Greeks tried (unlike us) to keep month and moon in step, despite occasional hitches (see note on p. 138).

Like a yo-yo: The text refers to tying a cockchafer to a thread by one foot and letting it buzz round as it tries to fly away.

You mean a burning-glass?: In the extant literature of the Classical period this is the only reference to the use of a lens for lighting a fire; and it reminds us how much we don't know about the details of Greek life.

Melt the wax: See the note on 'waxed tablets', p. 113.

By the Graces: The oath is appropriate to applause of a bright idea, since the Graces are a group of female deities who personify the attractiveness of works of art or admirable achievements.

And hang myself: Hanging was a very rare form of execution, but a very common form of suicide.

p. 145 **I'll throw him out of my house**: Strepsiades has tried that threat already (p. 117), and it did not work. This time the plot of the play requires that – combined with cajoling – it must work.

[To SOCRATES]: It may be that the first four verses are addressed to Strepsiades, reassuring him of the Clouds' favour (cf.

pp. 130 ff.), and the second four verses to Socrates; before 'Observe...' the Greek text has 'And you...', which suits a change of addressee.

p. 146   **In the name of Mist**: Strepsiades, as we see from much in this scene, has picked up miscellaneous ideas from his brief association with Socrates.

    Your uncle's pillared portico: A feature of large, costly houses.

    Promise you'll never tell: Strepsiades imitates the student who admitted him to the school and warned him to treat its activities as 'mysteries'.

    Awhirl: See note on pp. 128 f.

    Diag – I mean Socrates: Diagoras of Melos had earned notoriety – and the unenviable status of an outlaw – by preaching atheism in vehement and comtemptuous terms.

p. 147   **Getting their hair cut**: Pheidippides too wears his hair long (p. 112), but there is a difference between stylish long and neglected long.

    Getting ready for my funeral: An old English proverb says 'If it weren't for funerals and feasts, men would be dirty beasts'. The Greeks, by our standards, were.

    Get the court to certify him: If a young man could satisfy a lawcourt that his father was insane, he could be granted control of the family estate.

p. 148   **Lost your coat**: Strepsiades had to take it off before entering the school (pp. 133 f.) and evidently Socrates kept it.

    Pericles style: According to an anecdote reproduced in Plutarch (*Pericles* 23.1), when Pericles' accounts came up for scrutiny after the crushing of the Euboean revolt, a very large sum was allocated simply to 'necessary purposes'; the assembly, recognising that it had been spent in buying off the Spartan king at a moment of great danger for Athens, was content to ask no awkward questions.

    Do what I ask you...all right?: I prefer the translation 'And, what's more, do wrong' (*sc.* assuming that it is, as you think, wrong) 'in obedience to your father', i.e. 'However wrong it may be, please do it for *me*!'

    My very first obol of jury pay: A juror was paid three obols (half a drachma) for each day that he served.

    Hyperbolus did manage to learn it: This, of course, is not an allegation that Hyperbolus was actually taught public speaking by a sophist; comic poets are not historians. 6000 drachmas (one 'talent') is a very large sum indeed; Plato (*Apology* 20B) mentions 500 drachmas as the fee charged by Euenus of Paros for a course.

p. 149   **And they'll teach him themselves**: The Greek text continues 'And

I shan't be here'. In comedy only four actors were normally available for speaking parts; of course, the same actor could take several parts, and there were 'extras' for silent (or children's) parts. Since Strepsiades and Pheidippides have to be present throughout the contest of Right and Wrong, so that Strepsiades may make his choice at the end and hand over Pheidippides, the actor who has played Socrates must be taken offstage to change into the mask and costume of Right or Wrong. He does not seem to have much time for the change, but, as an ancient commentator observed, we would have expected a choral song before Right and Wrong enter, as at the corresponding point at the beginning of the contest in *Frogs* (ll. 814 ff.). It looks as if Aristophanes discarded the song which stood here in the original production and did not compose a fresh one, as he would have had to do if he had completed the revision with the serious intention of producing the play again.

Enter RIGHT: The contest has certain formal features which recur in other comedies. (1) The contestants enter, quarrelling. (2) They are persuaded to debate. (3) The Chorus exhorts contestant A. (4) Contestant A makes his case, with interruptions from B. (5) The Chorus comments, and exhorts B to reply. (6) B makes his case, with interruptions from A. (7) One of the two contestants wins. An ancient commentator states that Right and Wrong were brought on as fighting-cocks in cages. There is no trace of that in anything that is said or done in the scene as we have it, and the idea may be derived from metaphors or similes used in the choral song which preceded the contest (see above) in the original version of the play.

Where is she?: The word Wrong used for 'Justice' is not the ordinary abstract noun but *Dike*, the name of the goddess who is Justice personified (*dike* also means 'lawsuit' and occurs in the Greek phrases for 'claim one's rights', 'get one's deserts', etc.).

p. 150   **For putting his father in chains**: Zeus overthrew and imprisoned his father Cronus. In Aeschylus' *Eumenides* (ll. 640 ff.) the Furies make the same point against Zeus, and Apollo's response is not an argument but an outburst of bad temper, just as here Right's response is 'Ugh, you make me puke'. It was not easy to justify Zeus; some preferred (e.g. Plato, *Republic* 378BC) simply to deny the truth of all stories which told of conflict between gods.

Out-of-time old bagpipe: Right may possibly be portrayed as an old man, but that does not necessarily follow from these words; see note on 'Methuselah', p. 129.

Young bugger: The Greeks in general thought it natural and normal that a man should be sexually aroused as much by handsome boys as by pretty girls. They did not censure the pursuer, but they expected a good boy not to submit, and they vilified and despised the male of any age who enjoyed submitting and sought to attract male pursuers, calling him *katapugon* ('a down-into-the-arse man') or *euruproktos* ('having a wide anus'). English usage does not make this strong social and moral distinction between the 'active' and the 'passive' partners in homosexual acts, so that the translations 'bugger', 'sod' and 'gay' can all be misleading; nor did the Greeks think of an individual as '*a* homosexual'.

That Mysian Telephus: In a myth used by Euripides for a well-known (but now lost) play, Telephus, king of Mysia, appeared disguised as a beggar in the camp of the Greek expedition on its way to Troy. Comic poets fastened on that beggar-king as a symbol of 'degenerate' novelty in the theatre.

p. 151   **The way you taught Athens' boys in bygone years**: There is a curious asymmetry in this contest between 'the Old Education' and 'the New Education'. Right talks about 'secondary' education, constituted by music, poetry and physical training, to which boys were sent by their fathers (education was neither compulsory nor free) after they had learned to read and write. Wrong, on the other hand, talks about 'tertiary' education, now becoming available for the first time, from the sophists, to leisured young men who had already been through the hands of the music-master and the gymnastics teacher. Strictly speaking, the two educations were not mutually exclusive or in competition, except perhaps in the last years of adolescence. But Right implies that the traditional education of boys is the only education needed; having been trained in traditional skills – with no occasion to question or discuss anything – they will continue, as young men, to exert themselves in wrestling and manly sports. He also implies that the new ideas adopted by young men are infecting boys and ruining discipline in school.

p. 152   **And on no account pressing their thighs together**: So as not to push up their genitals into full view. Right has an obsessive interest in boys' genitals, as we see from the rest of his speech ('torment us with desire', and so on). Aristophanes has chosen to portray him not as a perceptive man who can expose the shallowness of Wrong, but as a sentimentalist hankering after the good old days when boys played out correctly their role (so abundantly illustrated on Attic vases of the sixth and early fifth centuries) as sex-objects in homosexual courtship.

Putting in chromatic bits: We know very little about music in the

Classical period, but it appears from allusions in comedy that musical style was undergoing changes in the direction of elaboration.

The sort Phrynis introduced: A mid-fifth century lyre-player; we have a citation from the comic poet Pherecrates in which Music complains of what Phrynis has done to her.

Grasshopper brooches: Once fashionable at Athens, but out of fashion by the time of the Peloponnesian War (Thucydides I 6.3).

Ceceides: There is no reliable evidence on this man, but he was probably a poet.

The men who fought at Marathon: The Athenians defeated a Persian expedition at Marathon, on the east coast of Attica, in 490, ten years before the great Persian invasion of Greece. The 'Marathon fighters', of whom very few can still have been living at the time of *Clouds*, were regarded as embodying the greatness of Athens in the old days.

p. 153   **The Pan-Athenian dance**: The reference is to a dance with an infantry shield at the Panathenaic festival.

And the public baths too: Not only something of a luxury, but a centre of gossip.

Hippocrates' sons: Not the famous doctor, but one of several Athenians who bore that name.

Academe's Park: It was two generations later that Plato and his associates met to study philosophy in the area called *Akademia*.

p. 154   **A pretty little prick**: It is clear from vase-painting that a small penis was more admired than a large one.

And the e-lection: The Greek text says 'decree', a surprise substitution for the expected 'penis'. The point is the same as that made by the chorus-leader's promise to Strepsiades (p. 131), 'there will be nobody carries more resolutions'.

Antimachus' ways: A poet of that name is cursed in *Acharnians*, l. 1150, p. 101.

p. 155   **Heracles having a cold bath**: Popular belief regarded warm springs as created by gods for Heracles to refresh him after his monster-slaying exploits; such springs were called 'Heracles' baths'.

The word 'marketeer': The *agora* of a Greek city-state was its central place, where people met and did business in and around public buildings. Sometimes 'market' is a possible translation; but the word could also mean 'assembly' and 'public speech'. When Homer calls Nestor *agoretes* he means 'speaker'.

What got Peleus his knife: Peleus (like Joseph) resisted the advances of his host's wife and was then accused by her of trying to seduce her. His host exposed him defenceless in a place full of dangerous beasts, but the gods rewarded his virtue by giving him a slashing-sword for self-defence.

Hyperbolus, the lamp man: it seems that Hyperbolus owned a workshop in which lamps were made.

That Thetis married him: Zeus and Poseidon both wanted Thetis, one of the daughters of Nereus, who dwelt in the sea. Learning that it was fated that Thetis' son should be 'mightier than his father', the gods prudently agreed to give her to a mortal husband, and they chose Peleus. The child of Peleus and Thetis was Achilles; but Thetis found life among mortals disagreeable, and went back into the sea.

p. 156   **Look at Zeus**: Zeus, like other gods, succumbed very readily to sexual temptation, and abused his supernatural status and powers to have intercourse with many mortal women. The argument 'If even Zeus is overcome by sexual desire, how can you blame *me*, a mere mortal?' is actually used by Helen in Euripides' *Trojan Women*, ll. 948 ff.

The carrot and ashes treatment: An adulterer caught in the act could be killed by the offended husband, or confined until he paid compensation; or, to humiliate him and symbolize his 'feminization' and rape by the husband, his pubic hair was burnt off with hot ash and a root vegetable was forced up his anus.

Bugger's arse: See note on p. 150; in what follows, 'bugger' and 'gay' are both translations of *euruproktos*.

Our advocates: The reference is to men who were chosen by the state to help the prosecution in cases of public importance. They are treated by comedy as unpopular men.

Yes, they are: Right has to be defeated, since the plot requires that Pheidippides should be taught by Wrong, and his defeat is accomplished by crude ridicule of comedy's favourite targets.

p. 157   **What about our politicians?**: One of the functions of comedy is to express resentment against those who are in some way superior to the average member of the audience: tragic poets, intellectuals, politicians, generals – and, on occasion, gods. The notion that eminent politicians were 'passive partners' in their youth is especially popular (e.g. *Knights*, ll. 878 ff.).

Throws his coat at STREPSIADES and PHEIDIPPIDES: He says, literally, 'Take my coat, because I'm deserting to you'. It is to the side of Wrong that he is 'deserting', but the plural (in the Greek) 'you' suggests that he may be regarding the audience as all on that side, in which case he could run through and out of the audience's area. 'Take my coat' may refer to the school's appetite for people's clothing (pp. 119, 133, 148) or it may be addressed to no-one in particular and uttered simply as he throws off his coat (the *himation*, translated here 'coat', is a voluminous garment) in order to run, like a deserter seizing an opportunity.

Shall I take your son, or do you want to be taught yourself?: The translation has gone wrong here; the actual meaning is, 'Do you want to take your son away, or am I to teach him to speak?'. In the manuscripts of the play these words (and 'All right; I promise you...' below) are spoken by Socrates; but that is impossible (see note on p. 149), and a summary of the play derived from an ancient commentator recognises that Wrong must be the speaker.

You'll sing a less ecstatic tune: This passage (two lines in the Greek text, greatly expanded in the translation) sounds the first note of foreboding about what is to come.

p. 158   **We would like to tell you, judges**: This is in effect a 'second parabasis', of a kind found at a similar point in other plays. The Chorus, sustaining the role of clouds visiting Athens on the occasion of the festival, and blending that with its role as participant in a play, offers promises and threats to the judges. The judges were a group of ten men, one from each of the ten sections (*phulai*) into which the citizen-body was divided, picked by lot from a larger number put forward by the *phulai*.

'Would to heaven I were in Egypt': Where it very seldom rains; but there is a further point, 'at the ends of the earth, rather than here', because Egypt was far away and the Greeks had a very low opinion of its inhabitants.

p. 159   **Old and New**: This was the name of the last day of the month.

Paid their deposits into court: A necessary step in bringing a lawsuit; and if the prosecution was successful, the defendant had to reimburse the prosecutor.

Just as a token of my appreciation: The Greek text does not tell us what Strepsiades has brought, but it has the masculine form of the demonstrative 'this', not the neuter: a tunic, a sack of flour, a dog? All those nouns are masculine in Greek, but 'money' is not; and a tunic would suit the jokes about the school's need for clothes (pp. 119, 133, 148). The wording accompanying the gift avoids the indelicacy of a direct reference to payment.

p. 160   **Then raise aloft**: Strepsiades launches into solo song, like a character in tragedy at a moment of intense emotion.

p. 161   **Our lawgiver Solon**: The codification of Athenian law early in the sixth century was attributed to Solon, and 'the laws of Solon' commonly meant what we would call 'Athenian law', even though new laws went on being made after Solon's time. The democratic constitution of Classical times was the product of reforms in the time of Cleisthenes, two generations later than Solon, and of certain further reforms in the first half of the fifth century; but the Athenians liked to think of their democracy as very old, and therefore exaggerated the democratic tendency of the constitutional, civil and criminal laws codified by Solon.

Who taste the food for festivals: It is not clear whether the function of these officials (called *protenthai*, 'foretasters') was practical or ritual.

In order to make away with as much of the deposit money as possible: It is a common assumption of comedy that all administrative officials are greedy and corrupt.

p. 162 **How happy is Strepsiades**: Strepsiades calls his song an *enkomion* (our 'encomium'), and its opening is formulaic ('Happy art thou, O...' or 'Blessed is...').

Enter FIRST CREDITOR and WITNESS: From what he says, it sounds as if this creditor is not a professional money-lender, but a fellow-demesman and friend, who now regrets his helpfulness. It is however possible that Greek money-lenders, like those of other ages, professed to be generous benefactors, helpful to those unfortunately beset by financial problems, and that Aristophanes is satirizing this pretence.

The witness, like many characters who appear briefly in Aristophanes, has a silent part.

I must not put Athens to shame: This may be a joke at Athenian litigiousness (see note on p. 120), but the creditor is not over-anxious to sue until insulted by Strepsiades, and I am inclined to think that the humorous point is the way we pluck up courage to carry out difficult actions by invoking lofty but irrelevant principles.

The twelve hundred drachmas: This was the first debt Strepsiades had in his notebook (p. 113). There it was for a 'horse with the Q brand', here for an 'ash-coloured horse'. Not surprisingly, some manuscripts call the creditor 'Pasias', but there is nothing in the text itself to justify naming him; many characters in Aristophanic comedy are not named.

In a place of my choice: On the importance of oaths, see note on p. 129. It was felt that a man who might risk perjury in comfortable surroundings and 'on home ground' would be less likely to risk it in an awe-inspiring sanctuary or at an altar, where the god seemed closer.

p. 163   **Who thinks a triffen is called a trough**: Strepsiades recalls the lesson he learned (p. 140).

p. 164   **I wouldn't like that to happen to you**: Strepsiades adds the crowning insult of patronising compassion.

     Enter SECOND CREDITOR: This creditor speaks as if he has had an accident while driving a chariot, and that creates a link with Ameinias, to whom Strepsiades paid 300 drachmas for a chariot (p. 113); but he is not named in the text.

     Not one of Carcinus' gods, is it?: Carcinus was a tragic poet, and so was one of his sons, Xenocles. The creditor's utterance 'O cruel goddess...' is taken from a play of Xenocles. The humorous point of 'Carcinus' *gods*' is not clear; possibly Carcinus brought gods on stage more often than other poets, possibly even, on one occasion, a god lamenting.

     O cruel goddess: The two verses are modelled (except for the reference to the chariot) on verses from Xenocles' tragedy *Licymnius*. Licymnius was killed by Tlepolemus (hence Strepsiades' response), his half-brother, and the lament was uttered by his half-sister Alcmene.

     What you fell off was the proverbial donkey: 'You've fallen off a donkey' (*ap' onou*) was a joking way of saying 'You've gone out of your mind' (*apo nou*).

     Had your brain shaken up: The Greeks very often spoke as if they thought the heart and liver to be the seat of emotion and thought, but they could not help knowing how injury to the head affected people. A Hippocratic treatise refers to the disastrous effects of 'shaking' the brain.

p. 165   **Sucks up water from the ground**: The source of rain was understood at least by the sixth century, but not, perhaps, by the man in the street.

     You gelding!: Most of the manuscripts have *o samphora, samphoras* being a horse branded with the archaic letter *san*. The two oldest manuscripts, however, have *o Pasia* – giving the Second Creditor the name which, if we are to think of the creditors as having names at all, must belong to the First Creditor (see note on p. 162). This is an unusually striking example of mistaken editorial interference with the text in late antiquity.

p. 166   **Is he not in love with evil?**: This choral song now prepares us fully for the reversal of fortune which is about to befall Strepsiades.

Help, cousins!: Since membership of a deme was inherited on the father's side, and a man's estate was divided between his sons on his death, it would be common to have one's uncles and cousins living in the same deme.

Cicynnians: See p. 117.

Hitting your father: See Introduction, p. xiii.

p. 167 **Sack-arse!**: This abusive term occurs in a fifth-century graffito from the Agora; it obviously means 'much buggered'.

I do like these compliments: Pheidippides is modelling himself on Wrong (p. 150).

Which of the Arguments do you want?: Protagoras was said to have taught his pupils how to 'praise and blame the same thing' with equal force (a very salutary exercise), and Pheidippides offers his father a choice of sides in the debate; but he himself would hardly be comfortable defending traditional values.

Search hard for ways this argument to win: We now come to a second contest comparable in structure with the contest between Right and Wrong (see note on p. 149); Strepsiades presents narrative which turns into argument at the end, Pheidippides presents an argument which turns into furious dialogue. Each of the contestants is introduced by a short choral song and encouragement from the chorus-leader. The need to conform to the traditional structure of a comic contest makes it impossible for the Chorus to sustain the grim moralising tone of their song on p. 166. Perhaps that is why they break the dramatic illusion on p. 167 ('Of course you know...').

And sing something by Simonides: Singing songs by famous poets, to the accompaniment of the lyre, was a traditional after-dinner practice. Simonides was an outstanding lyric poet who died about 470.

'The Fleecing of Lamb-achus': The poem in question was about a famous wrestler called Krios (the name means 'ram') and how he was 'shorn', i.e. defeated.

p. 168 **Grinding corn or something?**: Before the invention of radio – and still today, in most parts of the world – people sang constantly while performing monotonous work. Plutarch (*Banquet of the Seven Sages* 14) quotes some verses from a song sung by women while grinding corn.

Take a myrtle branch in his hand: A traditional practice in after-dinner recitation or unaccompanied singing; one cannot play a lyre at the same time as holding a branch but Strepsiades asked Pheidippides to 'recite' (*lexai*, 'speak') some Aeschylus, not to sing Aeschylean lyrics.

Recite some Aeschylus: Aeschylus died over thirty years before this play, and he was regarded by the older generation as the great dramatist of 'the good old days', the poet of the men who had fought at Marathon.

He uses bloody mountains: So in *Frogs* (ll. 924, 1056 ff.) Aeschylus is ridiculed by Euripides for using enormous words.

Sleeping with his sister – his sister on both sides!: Intercourse between children of the same father but different mothers was not regarded as incest by the Greeks. The play in question is *Aeolus*, in which Aeolus' son and daughter commit incest and the daughter bears a child. In *Frogs* it is made a charge against Euripides that he put on stage immoralities which were indeed enshrined in myth but 'should have been passed over in silence'.

p. 169   **Take you outside**: Some Greek houses had outside latrines (*Thesmophoriazusae*, ll. 484 f.), but a character in *Ecclesiazusae* considers that 'anywhere will do in the dark' (ll. 320 ff.), and for small children it is likely that anywhere would do even in daylight.

p. 170   **'The son gets thumped, do you think the father shouldn't?'**: In Euripides' *Alcestis* Admetus, to whom Apollo has granted the right to escape the fated hour of his death if he can find someone else to die in his place, tries to persuade his old father to be the substitute. The father replies 'You like to see the light of day; do you think your father doesn't?'

But what is a law anyway?: The Greeks in the fifth century realised that the laws, conventions, usages and traditional attitudes (all denoted by the word *nomos*) of any given culture are not implanted by nature but reflect the history and circumstances of that culture. It seemed to them that this was demonstrated by the fact that so many usages approved by one culture are repugnant to another. The observation provoked interest in the question 'What is dictated by nature (*phusis*)?', and some adopted the axiom that what is natural must be right. They also tended to believe that any given *nomos* originated with an individual legislator or thinker at a precise point in time, on the analogy of decrees proposed and put to the vote in an assembly of citizens. Hence Pheidippides' words 'He must have persuaded his people...'.

Why don't you go the whole hog?: The simple old man punctures Pheidippides' argument as effectively as any philosopher could have done; why should the nature of a human being be equated with the nature of a chicken? And one could add that even if it were, no obligation to follow the dictates of nature can be proved; it may be that the whole point of morality and law is to help us cope with the devastating neutrality of nature.

Not according to Socrates it isn't: The sophist's pupil, rejecting the authority of his elders, takes refuge, without reasoning, in the authority of his teacher.

p. 171   **I think he's right**: This may not be quite as sanctimonious as it sounds – the point may be 'I was such a fool to send my son to the sophists that I deserve what's happened to me' – but its tone anticipates the coming passage of dialogue between Strepsiades and the Clouds, and the tone of the play is uncompromisingly moralistic from now on.

This is really too much!: There was no formal scale of sin which rated mother-beating worse than father-beating, but the Greeks were as repelled as we are by violence against the weak and helpless. It was felt also that the womb and the breast created the closest of all human bonds.

Off the Acropolis: The Greek text says 'into the Pit' (*barathron*), where the bodies of executed criminals were thrown unburied, outside the city.

No, not our fault: The Clouds are now revealed as true deities (like the sun and moon) who responded to Socrates' invocation (pp. 123 ff.) only in order to make an example of Strepsiades and to punish him not for acts which he had already committed but for his dishonest intentions.

p. 172   **Show disrespect to my teacher?**: See note on 'Not according to Socrates', p. 170.

The great paternal Zeus: There is room for disagreement about the original meaning of *patroios* ('paternal') as an epithet of Zeus (possibly 'whose worship has been handed down to us by our fathers'), but no doubt that Strepsiades here uses it to mean 'Zeus who is concerned with the proper relationship between fathers and sons', as Zeus *Xenios* means 'Zeus who is concerned with the proper relationship between hosts and guests'.

Awhirl is king now: See pp. 128 f.

Set my mind awhirl: The Greek text says 'because of this whirl'. The word *dinos*, 'whirl', is ambiguous, since it also means a round goblet. 'This' suggests that such a goblet may have stood outside the door of the school, just as a traditional 'herm' (see below) stood outside Strepsiades' front door.

Hermes: It was customary to have a square-section pillar outside the street door, topped by a head of Hermes (hence 'herm') and adorned with an erect penis.

Forgive me: Greek gods are not very forgiving, but that does not prevent mortals from asking them for forgiveness.

And burn the blighters' school: The god's advice is in effect 'never mind about law, destroy them'; see Introduction, p. xiii.

Xanthias!: A common slave's name in comedy, and not an Athenian citizen's name. It is almost certainly derived from *xanthos*, 'fair-haired'.

p. 173   *CHAEREPHON*: See note on p. 116. If Chaerephon is to appear at all in the play (and we have just been reminded of him, p. 172), it should be in these last frantic moments, when all the inmates of the school are winkled out, and those manuscripts which give him a part here may well (by accident) be right. Given his gaunt, pale appearance (see note on p. 134) he might have been made identifiable by a portrait-mask.

I am walking upon air: The words of Socrates on p. 121.

p. 174   **The back side of the moon**: In the Greek, 'the *Hedra* of the moon', a word which can mean both 'established place' and 'rump', like the English 'seat'.

On them! Stones!: The words used (literally 'pursue, strike, throw!') are those used in a charge on the battlefield.

Let's go...has not been bad today: A lame ending, to our way of thinking; but with no stage-curtain or switching-off of lights, the end of a Greek comedy is often signalled in words. *Thesmophoriazusae* ends with similar self-reference by the Chorus. It is easier when the 'hero' of the play is departing in triumphal procession, followed by the Chorus, as in *Acharnians, Peace* and *Birds*.

Acharnians

The first character we meet in the prologue (ll. 1-203, pp. 49-58) is
Dikaiopolis, an Athenian farmer, who has been forced by the annual
invasions of the Peloponnesians to withdraw from his farm in the
country to the safety of the city of Athens. He sits alone on the Pnyx,
(one of the three major hills of the city just to the West of the
Acropolis), awaiting the arrival of his fellow citizens for the meeting
of the assembly. Like other heroes in Aristophanic prologues, and like
ourselves, he complains as he waits. He remembers incidents which
have brought him joy as well as those that angered him.

When the meeting is convened it is addressed by four speakers
other than Dikaiopolis, whose remarks are largely asides. First
Amphitheus, whose sanity is suspect not only because he claims divine
ancestry but also because he proposes peace with Sparta, is briefly
heard and then removed from the meeting. Next an ambassador
introduces a messenger from the King of Persia named Pseudartabas.
His one-eyed mask and nonsensical speech make him highly comic.
Finally we meet Theorus, an ambassador to Sitalces the King of
Thrace, whose soldiers steal Dikaiopolis' garlic. The hero is
unprotected by the members of the Council. Thus isolated he resolves
to take matters into his own hands.

The incidents serve to show how the assembly treats as a
complete fool anyone who suggests a treaty with the Spartans, but is
ready to accept the squandering of resources on pointless missions by
people who are more obviously misguided. Since the State shows no
interest in concluding a peace Dikaiopolis decides to do this for
himself. In the play Aristophanes deals with several issues that he was
to return to many times during his career, of which two are here given
prominence; the desire that peace prevail between the Greek States
and that the efficiency of the Athenian constitution should not be
impaired by those who sponged off the system.

p. 49 **Dikaiopolis:** A name formed from two Greek words: *dikaios*
'just' and *polis* 'city', 'state' or its 'people'. Dikaiopolis, in seeking

31

peace, acts as any 'just city' ought, and he appears in the play to be the only individual ('just citizen') with the common sense to see what is needed. (For a discussion of further implications in the name cf. E.L. Bowie *JHS* 108 (1988) p. 183). It is worth noting that our hero's name (as may often happen in Comedy) is not revealed to the audience until later (cf. l. 406, p. 67).

When Cleon coughed up his thirty thousand drachs: Dikaiopolis gleefully (coining a word, 'pleasurific') recalls an incident involving Cleon. According to the scholia the thirty thousand drachmas referred to here had been offered to Cleon as a bribe by certain tribute-paying allies of Athens in order that he might propose a reduction of their tribute. The 'Knights' (cavalry), who at this time represented the property-class of Athenian citizens who were wealthy enough to own their own horses, opposed Cleon and are said to have demanded the money from him. It is unlikely that this refers to an actual event (a conviction for bribery would have been a serious setback to Cleon's career); more probably, since the context is a theatrical one (cf. lines 9-16), this refers to an incident from comedy, perhaps from *Babylonians*.

Aeschylus: Together with Sophocles and Euripides he was a tragedian of highest repute. He had died in 456 BC, but a mark of the esteem in which he was held is the fact that his plays uniquely continued to be produced, although contemporary practice was not to do so. His poetry is parodied in *Frogs* as high-flown and ponderous but nonetheless it is clear that both there and here Aristophanes reveres him greatly. Theognis was an inferior tragic poet (cf. p. 55 and *Thesm.* l. 170).

Moschus and Dexitheus: Although little is known about either, we presume that Dexitheus was the superior of the two (it is recorded that he won a musical competition at the Pythian Games), as Aeschylus was to Theognis. We do not know what constituted a Boeotian tune. The lyre and the *aulos* (or double pipe) were commonly used for the accompaniment of choruses, including those of tragedy and comedy.

Soap: An alkali dust was used in the place of soap. The stinging of the soap is to be understood metaphorically of Dikaiopolis' anger. For similar metaphorical reference to anger cf. *Lys.*, ll. 295-6 (p. 191) and 1025-6 (p. 223).

p. 50   **The Market Square**: The *Agora* was the market place and city centre, where many of the city's religious and public buildings were. The people were ushered to the meetings of the assembly on the Pnyx by slaves employed as policemen who cleared the Agora with a red dyed rope. Anyone who tried to dodge the rope but was marked by it was liable to a fine.

The Executive Committee: Sessions of the assembly were guided by an executive committee called the *Prytaneis*, whose duty it was to prepare and direct the business of the meeting. The *Prytaneis* were one tenth of a larger administrative body known as the *Boule* or Council; each set of *Prytaneis* was given the responsibility of presiding for thirty-six successive days of the year. The *Boule* consisted of five hundred members annually chosen by lot.

My heart's in the fields: Dikaiopolis, a farmer, from the deme of Cholleidae (p. 67) longs to be back in the country. The war with the Peloponnesians had resulted in the abandonment of Attica and the retreat of all those who lived outside the city to the safety of Athens.

For sale: The Greek has a pun which is difficult to translate into English. The word *prio*, which is the cry of the vendor to 'buy' his produce, is rendered as if it were the name of the man. This man, says Dikaiopolis, whose piercing cries were unheard of before the war, is now a frequent visitor to the market. The ravaging of the Attic countryside devastated the harvests and necessitated the import of food. Dikaiopolis is annoyed that he has to endure the unpleasantness of the city no less than its marketeering. His annoyance is given expression in the pun upon the word *prion* (a saw) which suggests that this man's voice is rasping.

Come forward...the consecrated enclosure!: These are probably the words of the official opening of the assembly. Preparatory to business a sacrifice was held and the blood of the victim was used to demarcate and sanctify the boundaries of the assembly area.

Amphitheus: The name literally translates 'divine on both sides', but it may be that of an actual Athenian. The genealogy combines known names of both divinities and mortals, which prompts the joke question 'Are you human?'. In view of this the name is probably invented.

Who wishes to speak?: Again the official words preparatory to an address to the assembly. Any citizen was permitted to speak.

p. 51   *Scythian archers*: These were public slaves who policed the city under the authority of magistrates.

The Persian Court!: The luxury of the Persian Court had become proverbial. From Persia peacocks had recently been introduced to Greece. The magnificence and opulence of the Persian ambassadors will have been absurdly over-exaggerated. They may well have closely resembled peacocks themselves.

p. 52   **Ecbatana**: Media's capital city and the summer residence of the Great King is used here as an expletive.

The year when Euthymenes was archon: Of the nine archons at Athens who held office for one year the Eponymous Archon gave his name to the year. Euthymenes held this position in 437/6 BC. The ambassadors are imagined as having lived at public expense for eleven years. They have taken their time to complete their mission and pretend that they have had to endure great hardships.

Cayster valley: The river Cayster flowed from Sardis and entered the sea at Ephesus. The way from Ephesus to Sardis along the flood plain of this river formed the first part of the journey to the Great King's court. The Royal Road extended from Sardis to Sousa allowing swift communication between the East and the West of the Empire.

Among the rubbish on the city walls!: The walls of Athens not only encircled the city but also connected it to its seaport, Piraeus. Thucydides records (cf. II 17) how the people were crowded into the city as a result of the yearly invasions of the Spartans and their allies. Some, he says, found billets in the towers of the walls. In 430 BC a terrible plague broke out in the city which was made worse, though not caused, by the over-crowding and inevitable resultant lack of hygiene. The plague broke out again in 427 BC (cf. Thuc. III 87). The effects of the overcrowding will have been much in the people's minds. No doubt they feared further recurrences.

Only sweet wine, and even refused to put any water in it: The sweetness of wine was a mark of its quality. Poor wines quickly became acidic. Generally the Greeks mixed their wine with water; not to do so was intemperate and the mark of a 'barbarian', i.e., a non-Greek.

Cecrops: In myth he was the first king of Athens.

How many you can lay: In comedy politicians are commonly demeaned by reference to their alleged sexual deviancy (cf. *Knights*, ll. 423-8, 878-80; *Clouds*, ll. 1093-4, p. 157; *Eccl.*, ll. 112-13). The Greek is much more explicit than the translation, suggesting that politicians are the passive partners of the homosexual act. Such a role was far less socially acceptable than the 'active' practice of homosexuality (cf. *Clouds*, note p. 150).

To the jakes: The king is engaged on a visit to the 'golden hills' (which were proverbially made from solid gold) in 'some out of the way part' of Persia. Yellow in Greek terms is the colour of faeces and so the 'out of the way place' becomes the toilet.

Oxen baked whole in the oven: According to Herodotus (I 133.1) on special occasions Persian princes would serve whole oxen or horses or camels or asses roasted in an oven. Aristophanes' word *kribanos*, meaning a small bread oven, is deliberately ridiculous.

p. 53
Cleonymus: He is persistently satirized by Aristophanes, firstly for his obesity (*Wasps*, l. 592) and secondly for the cowardice he allegedly showed when he discarded his shield as he fled from the battle of Delium (*Clouds*, l. 352, p. 127). Otherwise he is known as a politician who was the author of several decrees concerning the enforcement and collection of tribute from the Athenian allies.

A bezzle: *Phenax* is used as if the name of a bird but actually implies that Cleonymus is a cheat. The word *phenakizein* 'to cheat' appears in the next line.

Pseudartabas: His name combines the word *pseudes* 'false' with *artabe*, a Persian measure. Here is another who will cheat the assembly.

The King's Eye: This was indeed the title of a Persian official (Herodotus I 114.2).

You look like a bloody battleship: Pseudartabas is presumably wearing a mask with one gigantic eye. Thus Dikaiopolis compares him to a ship with an eye painted on its bow. 'Why, you've even got an oar-pad', says Dikaiopolis, extending the comparison with a ship. He is probably comparing the bags under the ambassador's eye or the beard around his mouth with the leather covers which prevented water splashing through the lower oar-holes of a ship.

Yartaman esharsha: Pseudartabas speaks gibberish which is meant to sound like Persian.

Yawonian: This is Pseudartabas' pronunciation of 'Ionian'. The Athenians, as also the islanders of the Aegean and many of the Greek inhabitants of Asia Minor, were of the Ionian 'race'. The Spartans were from another immigration of peoples into Greece known as the Dorians. There is probably no intention to distinguish the races here but a general reference, since the Persians called all Greeks 'Ionians'. From Herodotus (I 143.3) we learn that the Athenians did not like to be called Ionians.

Sack-arsed: The Athenians are described as 'wide-arsed' (*khauno-proktos*) because they indulge in anal intercourse. To Dikaiopolis the abuse is clear, but the ambassador claims that Pseudartabas had said *akhanas* (a Persian measure, which the translation takes to be a sackful) and that Dikaiopolis had misheard him.

p. 54
Lydian purple: The Greek has 'Sardian purple', Sardis being the

capital of the former Lydian kingdom. It was now one of the major cities of the Persian Empire and the seat of the Satrap (provincial governor). The luxuries for which the Imperial courts were well known would have included garments dyed purple. Phoenician purple, as it was also known, was a very expensive commodity. Dikaiopolis is in effect saying 'I'll beat you black and blue' or 'I'll give you a bloody nose'.

Cleisthenes: The attendants of Pseudartabas to whom Dikaiopolis points are eunuchs. Castration was not practised in Greece but this provides the opportunity for a joke about the effeminacy of Cleisthenes who is mockingly called the son of 'Athletes'. (In the Greek Cleisthenes is said to be the son of Sibyrtius, an owner of a wrestling school. It is possible that Cleisthenes was his son but more likely that the reference is sarcastic.) By a few word changes the next lines, firstly from Euripides and then from the iambic poet Archilochus, become further slurs upon Cleisthenes' character. Cleisthenes' beardless state is also ridiculed elsewhere in Aristophanic comedy (*Knights*, ll. 1373-4; *Clouds*, l. 355, p. 127). Strato was also thought effeminate and is mentioned together with Cleisthenes at *Knights*, l. 1374.

In the City Hall: This was known as the *Prytaneion*. Here the presiding council (see note on the Executive Committee, p. 50) met and entertained visiting embassies at public expense.

Eight drachmas: A skilled labourer might expect to be paid one drachma a day.

p. 55   **Sitalces of Thrace**: This king had become an ally of Athens early in the war. He had launched an attack upon neighbouring Macedonia, expecting Athenian help but had been unsupported and failed (Thuc. II 95-101). Since it was important for Athens to keep on best terms with her allies in Northern Greece, doubtless many embassies will have been sent to ensure continued allegiance.

Theorus: He became a favourite butt of Aristophanic jokes. (cf. *Clouds*, l. 400, p. 129; *Wasps*, ll. 42-51, 418-19, 1236-42). He was often associated with Cleon.

Theognis: cf. note p. 49 above. He is described as frigid because (if Aristophanes is to be believed) his work was so boring. A single Greek word translates both adjectives. Theorus comments that it was cold in Thrace at exactly the time it was cold in Athens, i.e. when Theognis was producing his plays.

The Festival of the Clans: The Apaturia was an Athenian festival at which the children of citizens were admitted to their clan. The clan was a religious association of families upon membership of which Athenian citizenship depended. Sadocus the son of Sitalces was given the exceptional honour of being granted Athenian citizenship when in 431 BC an agreement between Sitalces and Athens was made (Thuc. II 29). Sausages were a delicacy at this festival.

p. 56   **The Odomantian Army**: The Odomantians were a Thracian tribe whom Aristophanes wrongly supposes to have served under Sitalces (cf. Thuc. II 101.3).

Who cut the leaf off your fig?: The verb *apothriazo* is used specifically of stripping fig leaves but is used here to imply circumcision. Dikaiopolis' examination of the soldiers' phalluses will have been more than sufficiently explicit.

Two drachmas a day: This is a high rate of pay for a soldier. Half this wage would have been more usual (cf. Thuc. VII 27 where Thracian peltasts are paid one drachma. Two drachmas were paid to the hoplites at Potidaea (III 17). This is mentioned by Thucydides as a squandering of Athenian resources).

Boeotia: This was the neighbouring federation of states to the North of Attica, dominated by Thebes.

The oarsmen who saved Athens from the Medes: Since the Athenian navy was so strong, the oarsmen who manned the fleet and who themselves were only paid one drachma a day constituted a powerful lobby in Athenian politics. The maritime power of Athens had proved itself in defeating the Persian fleet at Salamis in 480 BC. 'From the Medes' is not in the Greek and the reference is probably to the present rather than to the past – 'The oarsmen who save Athens'.

The stuff makes them run wild: From *Knights* (ll. 494, 946) we learn that garlic was fed to cocks to increase their ferocity.

Zeus has sent a sign: It was possible to get an adjournment of the assembly in the event of a 'sign from Zeus'. An earthquake (Thuc. V 45.4) or thunder (*Eccl.*, l. 792) might constitute such a sign. A few spots of rain are a sufficient excuse for Dikaiopolis and in this case the *prytaneis*.

Dikaiopolis sadly gathers up the remains of his lunch and walks off: A revolving stage which is suggested in the translation is a modern device for representing such a scene change. Changes of scene in Greek theatre are imagined rather than actual. It is not clear when the scene changes except that at line 202 Dikaiopolis says that he is about to go inside. The central door of the *skene* must be imagined to represent Dikaiopolis' house. Nor is it clear where Dikaiopolis meets Amphitheus, whether before his house or at the deserted Pnyx.

All O.K.? Not yet: Dikaiopolis greets Amphitheus with the word *khaire* which usually simply means 'hello'. Amphitheus replies 'not yet' making a pun on the word's literal meaning 'rejoice'. His return from Sparta is remarkably swift. He was only sent at lines 130-2, pp. 54-5, cf. *Lys.* note pp. 225-6.

Acharnians: The largest of the *demoi* (townships), Acharnae was in central Attica, North-west of Athens. Since it supplied the largest number of soldiers and voters it was severely plundered by the Spartans (cf. Thuc. II 20). Nevertheless the Acharnians showed a remarkable resilience and desire for vengeance, hence the description 'close-grained oak and maple'. It is these people that Dikaiopolis must persuade if he wants peace.

These three peaces: Amphitheus carries with him three wine-skins which he refers to as 'three peaces'. The Greek *sponde* is both a 'treaty' and a 'libation', because agreements were ratified by the pouring of a libation. Peace and wine are thus significantly associated. By contrast, war and wine are opposed, since the invasions of the Spartans had meant the destruction of the Attic vines. These ideas become thematic and recur significantly at the end of the play (cf. pp. 94-5).

Real men of Marathon: The battle of Marathon fought against the Persians in 490 BC marked a significant moment in Greek history and, judging from subsequent art and literature, a turning point in Athenian self-confidence. At the battle the Athenians had withstood the might of a Persian army without the support of the Spartans. The Acharnians, who are said to be veterans of Marathon, are as uncompromising now as they were then, despite the fact that they would have been over eighty years old at least if they were still alive at the time of this production.

Five years: This refers to the duration of the treaty, but also suggests the maturity of the wine.

It simply reeks of turpentine and shipyards: Pitch was used both to flavour wine and to seal the hulls of ships.

Trying to get the allies to send troops: The allies of Athens, here in the Greek called simply 'the states', were mostly in fact tribute-paying vassals, and their relationship with Athens was not always cordial. The acidity of the wine reflects the bitterness of the relationship, not least because some of the subject-states were forced to provide ships for the war. The majority, however, provided money. Neither the five year nor the ten year peace will do, since they would merely provide both sides with the opportunity of replenishing their losses before renewing the struggle.

p. 58 **Thirty years, by land and sea**: A peace for thirty years had been concluded at the end of the First Peloponnesian War in 446/5 BC. When terms were drawn up between Sparta and Athens four years after the production of this play, they were intended to be effective for fifty years (Thuc. V 18). Dikaiopolis enjoys the taste of the more enduring wine and likens it to the fabled drink of the gods, nectar and ambrosia.

'Come prepared with rations for three days': This was the order given at levies of troops.

The Country Dionysia: The City Dionysia was held in the spring at Athens and attracted many to its festivities, notably to its dramatic competitions. Various local communities held similar celebrations on a smaller scale in or about December, but since the outbreak of the war Dikaiopolis has not been able to celebrate these in his own deme.

The entry of the chorus is termed the *Parodos*, and regularly follows an initial scene where the plot of the play has been loosely established. Here the members of the chorus, who like other choruses give their name to the play, are charcoal burners from Acharnae. True to their reputation (cf. note p. 57) they are incensed that someone has dared to make peace with the Spartans (cf. Thuc. II 20-1). Thucydides tells us that the Acharnians, when they saw their lands being ravaged by the Peloponnesian army in the first year of the war, wanted to march out against the enemy. That bellicose spirit is reflected here. They enter the circular dance floor in front of the stage in excited agitation looking for the man who has betrayed his country.

Meanwhile Dikaiopolis, who has secured a private peace, is preparing to celebrate his return to the country. He leads in procession his daughter, who carries items for the sacrifice, and two slaves, who hold up a phallic symbol. He is intending to celebrate the Country Dionysia (cf. note above) but he is prevented from enjoying these revelries by the chorus who threaten to stone him.

The scene must now be imagined to be before Dikaiopolis' house, where he is making preparations for his celebrations. Previously the Pnyx had been the setting for the dramatic action. The change, and that to Euripides' house, was not clarified by the removal and replacement of scenery but was imagined.

The effectiveness of the scene owes something to the juxtaposition of the chorus' urgency with the mock solemnity of Dikaiopolis' procession and much to the flippancy with which the ritual of sacrifice is treated.

p. 59   **Keep silent all!**: Holy rites were commonly respectfully observed, if not in silence, at least with auspicious words. Dikaiopolis uses a regular exhortation preparatory to his sacrifice (cf. *Clouds*, l. 236, p. 123).

Xanthias: Many slaves in Aristophanic comedy are given this name. The name in Greek suggests one who has fair rather than black hair; a mark of a non-Greek.

p. 60   *Taking a cake out*: Cakes (more like thin wafers than our own cakes) were sacrificially offered to the gods, as were drink offerings.

O Lord Dionysus: Dionysus, the god of wine, is appropriately invoked, being the god in whose honour the Country Dionysia was celebrated. Dikaiopolis, whose peace will secure his return to the country and to his vines, hails the god who protects these.

Pretend you've got horseradish in your mouth: Various other bitter herbs were also substituted to complete the saying ('a savory/horseradish-eating look') and imply a sour expression. Young girls should not be seen coyly smiling, gossiping or laughing during solemn religious rites.

Little kittens: The Greek has 'polecats'. They are not as lovable as kittens but were kept for the practical purpose of catching mice.

p. 61   **Phales**: The phallus which is carried in front of Dikaiopolis' procession is thus personified. It was a common enough symbol of fertility and was associated with various rites, not least with the Country Dionysia. Dikaiopolis playfully associates Phales with the joy of raping a neighbour's slave-girl. In effect he is celebrating a return to wine (Bacchus) and women (Phales) which he supposes peace will bring.

Lamachus: He was a well known fighter and general, who is chosen because he typifies those who favoured the continuation of the war (cf. *Peace*, ll. 304, 473-4, 1290-4). As a general in 424 BC he led a naval squadron in the Black Sea (Thuc. IV 75) and was later to be appointed jointly to the command of the Sicilian expedition. He was also one of those who swore to the Peace of Nicias in 421 BC. Perhaps he is chosen because of his name; *mache* meaning 'battle'.

A potful of peace: Aristophanes continues the idea that peace can be drunk (cf. note on 'these three peaces', p. 57) and so makes a surprise substitution of 'peace' for 'soup'; soup being the more usual Greek remedy for a hangover.

The chorus burst upon the scene at line 280, scattering the procession.

Lyric metres accompany this moment of high excitement. Dikaiopolis tries to quell the onslaught of the chorus, but they are eager to stone the traitor and their cries are those of battle (cf. Xenophon, *Anabasis* V 7.21). There follows a dialogue between Dikaiopolis and the chorus leader (p. 63), in which the former tries to convince the latter that in seeking peace he has acted rationally. When reason fails, Dikaiopolis seizes a basket of charcoal (a commodity for which the Acharnians were famous) and threatens his hostage with a knife. The absurdity of treating an object as a human being is commonplace in comedy, but is heightened in this instance by the parody of Euripides' *Telephus* which it involves.

p. 62   **It'll be your turn next year**: A more accurate rendering of the Greek finds the chorus threatening Cleon with being 'cut up into leather soles to make shoes for the Knights'. This is appropriate treatment for a son of a tanner and a bitter adversary of the 'Knights' (cf. l. 6, p. 49). The translation adds a further twist by supposing a reference to the play Aristophanes staged in the next year, namely *Knights*. The aside from the chorus at this point in the play is not common, being more usual in the *parabasis* (cf. Sommerstein intro. pp. 26-7), but it demonstrates the thin line upon which the dramatic illusion was based.

p. 63   **With my head on the block ...you can decapitate me on the spot!**: Here and in the scenes that follow Aristophanes parodies the plot and speeches of Euripides' *Telephus*. In this play Telephus the king of the Mysians enters the Greek camp dressed as a beggar. This he does in order to receive healing for a wound from the very man who had inflicted the injury, for an oracle had declared that this was his only hope of cure. In an address to Agamemnon Telephus says, 'No, not even if a man with an axe in his hand were about to strike my neck, I will not keep silent'. The absurdity of Aristophanes' parody is that this is taken literally. Decapitation was not in fact a Greek punishment; so the block is not the executioner's block.

Let's paint him red!: This English metaphor replaces a Greek one, 'to card him into a scarlet cloak', the implication being that someone is going to be beaten bloody. Since scarlet seems to have been a common colour for Spartan attire (see *Lys.*, l. 1140, p. 227), the traitor's treatment is most appropriate.

The charcoal in your hearts has blazed up: Dikaiopolis counters the bloody 'red' metaphor with his own, which makes reference to the blackness with which the Acharnians were associated because of their production of charcoal (cf. also *Lys.* note p. 192 'I think a mad dog').

p. 64   **I will kill your nearest and dearest**: At this point we do not know what hostage Dikaiopolis has seized. The surprise is that this is a basket of charcoal (cf. l. 331). The scene is a parody of that in Euripides' *Telephus*, where Telephus secures his own life by seizing the son of Agamemnon. There is a similar parody in *Thesm.*, ll. 689-761.

    Common hum...common coality: A pun here depends upon the words *anthrakon* and *anthropon*; the one meaning 'of coals', the other 'of men'.

    You've still got some hidden away in those cloaks: No doubt the audience will have been keen to see what the chorus do have hidden beneath their cloaks!

p. 65   **Mount Parnes**: This range of mountains bordered Attica to the North and its foothills extended at least in part into the deme of Acharnae. The wooded slopes provided the source of charcoal for which the deme was famous.

Two short pieces sung by the chorus (ll. 358-63 and 385-90) enclose a speech of Dikaiopolis. The dochmiac rhythms that are used in these are rare in comedy but more common in tragedy where they are employed at moments of great emotion. The parody is fitting in view of the perilous situation in which Dikaiopolis and the author are about to place themselves, for the phrasing of line 367 and the use of the first person at line 377 suggest that Aristophanes is himself here speaking. Such a break in the dramatic illusion outside the *parabasis* where the chorus leader often becomes the mouthpiece of the author is not common (cf. ll. 654-64, p. 78). It is improbable that Dikaiopolis would have put on a bald wig to make clear any resemblance to the author as the stage direction suggests.

p. 66   **And the senior citizens, who serve on juries**: Since the pay for jury service was substantially below that which could be earned by a manual worker (2 obols were paid before 423 BC, when 3 obols were introduced by Cleon) it was little more than pocket-money and certainly not enough to feed a family. This being so the courts were largely attended by the old. This is satirized by Aristophanes in *Wasps* where the jurors are wasp-like because of their vicious sting. The metaphor of stinging or biting (cf. l. 376) may have been proverbial.

    I know that better than anyone: Aristophanes is here speaking for himself through Dikaiopolis. He had been accused by Cleon after the production of *Babylonians* in the previous year (426 BC) of 'slandering the city in the presence of foreigners'. In *Acharnians* he is careful to avoid such accusations (cf. ll. 504-8 and 513-15, pp. 71-2), for, as he says, he 'very nearly drowned' (ll. 381-2, p. 66).

He dragged me into the Council Chamber: The accusation was probably in the form of an *eisangelia* which applied to cases where no specific law had been contravened. Such matters were first brought before the Council who decided whether there was a case to answer.

His mouth spewed out a torrent: Cleon is elsewhere also referred to as a torrent (cf. *Wasps*, l. 1034 and *Knights*, l. 137).

To dress up properly for my trial: An appeal to the emotions could, at least judging from extant speeches and from what Aristophanes says in *Wasps*, be as effective as a careful presentation of the facts. Aristophanes takes what is accepted and understood from daily life and exaggerates. This results in a highly comic and poignant episode which is made all the more humorous for being a clever parody of the Euripidean *Telephus*.

Hieronymus: The chorus are wise to Dikaiopolis' attempt to escape by using an over-emotional appeal and therefore draw a comparison with Hieronymus, a tragic poet whose stage characters cut a very pathetic appearance and whose plays were excessively emotional. He may well himself have shared something in common with his characters for if the scholion is right at *Clouds*, l. 349 to identify 'the son of Xenophantus' with Hieronymus then our tragic poet was notable for his unkempt appearance ('a wild man...one of those hairy sex maniacs', *Clouds*, p. 127). He is said to wear 'an invisibility hat' since he cannot be identified through his mop of hair. The chorus in effect say that even were Dikaiopolis to present himself as Hieronymus or one of his characters they still would not be moved by his appeal for mercy.

All the tricks from Sisyphus' store: Homer called Sisyphus 'the craftiest of all men' (*Iliad* VI 153). Theognis (ll. 701-4) tells how he tried to cheat death. The chorus leader warns the Acharnians to beware of such trickery.

In order to win the pity of the chorus, Dikaiopolis proposes to dress as a beggar. Therefore he goes to the house of Euripides to ask for the rags of Telephus (cf. note p. 68). The ensuing scene gives the comic poet the opportunity to parody both Euripidean drama and tragedy in general. Dikaiopolis' approach is like that of a real beggar at a rich man's door, but the fact that he begs for beggar's clothes and that his requests become increasingly disrespectful make the scene comic.

Aristophanes was often to return to making fun of Euripides; his intellectualism, his paradoxical language and in particular his unconventional approach to tragedy.

He goes to Euripides' house and knocks: Euripides' door will have been represented by the central door of the *skene*. When the tragic poet appears he is rolled out on the *ekkyklema*; a trolley usually used to represent a scene taking place inside the building.

p. 67 **Cephisophon**: According to *Frogs*, ll. 944 and 1452 this actor and friend of Euripides assisted the great master in the writing of his plays. It is highly likely that Cephisophon's name has been mistakenly added (for he was not a slave, cf. l. 401) by an ancient commentator where the manuscripts have no speaker indicated. This also happens elsewhere in comedy as in the case of the creditors in *Clouds* (cf. note p. 162).

He is and is not: This is typical of the paradoxical statements found in Euripidean plays (cf. *Alcestis*, l. 521; *Iphigenia in Tauris*, l. 512, *Troades*, l. 1223), which may reflect a sophistic influence.

His mind is not at home...but he himself is at home: Again there is the paradox already noted above with the additional, absurdly satirical, idea of composing while being out of one's mind (cf. *Ion*, l. 251, 'Though I was here, I must have had my mind back at home').

Upstairs: The same word translated here as 'upstairs' can also be rendered 'with one's feet up', as the scholion recognizes. The staging of the scene will be effected by the choice we make (cf. note below on 'I am too busy to come downstairs').

Euripikins: The diminutive would have been an affectionate form of address to a child, but here, as at *Clouds*, p. 121, it is wheedling.

Cholleidae: This is the deme to which Dikaiopolis belongs.

From inside, on the top floor: This stage direction supposes that we have understood 'upstairs' at line 399. The 'mechanical gubbins' might then be the *deus ex machina*, which was used to lower gods from an upper storey on to the stage. But 'I'm coming round' conceals a pun on the word *ekkuklema*, the stage device used to 'roll out' an interior scene. Euripides will appear through the central door of the *skene* rolled out on this device. The Greek theatre did not have a revolving stage. It is best then to delete 'on the top floor' and change Dikaiopolis' question to 'Why not roll yourself out?'.

I am too busy to come downstairs: In view of what has been said above this is best taken as 'too busy to get down from my couch'.

p. 68 **What sayest thou?**: Euripides speaks as if he were a character from one of his own tragedies, or as if he can only talk in tragic diction.

Now I know why you put so many cripples in your plays: Since he cannot even get himself down from his couch and has to be wheeled out, it is little wonder that the heroes he creates are lame. For similar accusations against Euripides of creating cripples and beggars cf. *Frogs*, ll. 842 and 1063-4.

One of your old plays: Dikaiopolis is thinking of one play in particular but cannot remember its title. The guessing game which follows heightens anticipation and reminds the audience of some Euripidean plays in which the heroes appeared as beggars.

I've got a long speech to make to the Chorus: Notice that he does not say, 'to the Acharnians'. For a similar breaking of the dramatic illusion cf. *Clouds* 326 and 1351-2.

Ill-fated Oeneus: King Oeneus appeared in Euripides' play of the same name as a beggar after having been deposed by his adversaries. He was reinstated to his rightful position by his grandson Diomedes.

Blind Phoenix: After having been cursed by his father for a misdemeanour with a slave girl, for which in the Euripidean version he was not responsible, Phoenix went into exile and blinded himself.

Philoctetes: A member of the Greek expedition to Troy, he was abandoned on the island of Lemnos because of the revulsion that a gangrenous snake bite caused amongst his companions. There the lame Philoctetes had to eke out a living alone.

Lame Bellerophon: This hero gave his name to another Euripidean play. In attempting to ride to heaven on the winged horse Pegasus he angered Zeus, who sent a gadfly to sting the steed. Bellerophon was crippled by his fall.

Mysian Telephus: His name the audience has long guessed, especially if they had understood the parodies of earlier lines (cf. ll. 318, 326). He was king of Mysia, a region which lies to the south of the Troad. In defending his country against the invading Greeks he was wounded by Achilles and could find no cure except by being obedient to the advice of an oracle which proclaimed that his wounder would also be his healer. In order to gain admission to the Greek camp he disguised himself as a beggar.

Thyestes: He suffered the hideous humiliation of unknowingly banqueting upon the flesh of his own children. This was the revenge taken upon him by his brother Atreus who discovered Thyestes' adultery with his wife. Thereafter he was forced to live in exile.

Ino: Supposed dead by her husband, but in fact revelling with a band of bacchants in the mountains, Ino was supplanted at the palace by a new wife. When the king found that his first wife was still living he smuggled her into the palace as a slave. Jealousy between the two wives led to the deaths of the children of both, except one, a son of Ino with whom she fled.

p. 69   **'O Zeus who seest through and under all!'**: This is probably a quotation from tragedy, although the source is unknown. It is aptly spoken as Dikaiopolis holds up the tattered garment.

'For I this day...but not appear myself': The lines according to the scholiast are from Euripides' *Telephus*.

The audience...the Chorus: Comedy does not hesitate to break the dramatic illusion (cf. l. 416).

'O be thou blest...': This again is a quotation from *Telephus* identified by the scholiast. Telephus speaks these lines to his Greek audience who do not see through his disguise. To the assembled Greeks his words appear to be a curse, but they are intended by the speaker to be a prayer for blessing. Dikaiopolis' plea for peace is well intentioned, but to the chorus it is treacherous.

You're making me quite poetic already: The tragic rags begin to take effect immediately. They seem to inspire Dikaiopolis magically.

Seest thou...and I haven't got half the things I came for: The tragic elegance of the first line is marred by the materialistic bathos of the next. For this common comic effect cf. *Lys.*, ll. 714-17, p. 210.

p. 70   **Just like your mother used to be!**: Dikaiopolis thanks Euripides but cannot leave without parting sarcasm. Rumour had it that Euripides' mother made a living by selling vegetables.

A little pot, with a hole in it: Possibly this mimics a container carried by Telephus in which he kept ointment for his wound.

Thou'lt rob me soon of all my tragic art: As if beggarly attire were all that comprised Euripidean tragedy. The new 'realism' introduced by Euripides in his depiction of men 'as they are' (Aristotle) is at issue in the argument between Aeschylus and Euripides in *Frogs*.

My very dearest Euripides: The seemingly never-ending requests of Dikaiopolis for 'just one more item' draw from Euripides' growing hostility. It is with increasing anticipation that the audience await the moment when Dikaiopolis will go too far and spur Euripides into losing his temper.

The parsley your mother left to you: cf. note on 'Just like your mother used to be' above. This really must be the final straw!

p. 71   **On your marks – set – go**: The Greek says 'there is the line'. The scholia take this to be the starting line but fifth-century usage (cf. *CQ* 28 [1978] 383) suggests that the finishing line is meant.

Now suitably attired for a speech which will parody that of

Telephus before the Greeks, Dikaiopolis presents to the chorus his reasons for having made peace with Sparta. The causes of the conflict between Athens and Sparta he imputes to the scurrilous motives of Pericles. Dikaiopolis claims that the Megarian Decree had been occasioned by a squabble over abducted prostitutes, in which Aspasia the mistress of Pericles was involved. He argues that the Spartans cannot be held entirely responsible for the outbreak of the war and that the issue of the Decree is a futile reason for war. The way in which Aristophanes chooses to make his point is largely fanciful. He uses parody of *Telephus* and of the opening of Herodotus' history (cf. Hdt. I 1-5), as well as lampooning the likes of Pericles and Aspasia. But one wonders to what extent the plea for peace (although humorous) is a serious one and to what extent the Decree was still an issue in 425 BC. There may well have been those who had opposed the necessity for war on account of the Megarian Decree in 432 BC (cf. Thuc. I 139.4) and who now in 425 BC protested their former good advice.

'Don't hold it against me, gentlemen': These words formed the opening of a famous speech of Telephus. The whole of Dikaiopolis' speech is very probably modelled on this. For the audience to be able to appreciate the parody the Telephean speech must have been well known at least in parts. After dinner recitals and an oral education will have ensured that many were well versed (cf. *Clouds*, ll. 1365 ff., p. 168).

Not even a comedian can be completely unconcerned with truth and justice: Aristophanes himself speaks at this point, reminding the audience in the lines that follow of his prosecution at the hands of Cleon (cf. notes to p. 66). In claiming to speak with truth and justice he steps momentarily outside the persona of Dikaiopolis.

With tribute or with troops: Athens collected tribute from her subject-allies on a yearly basis and levied troops from some of them. Originally the purpose was to oppose the Persians but gradually reserves were used against Greek enemies. From this passage and from Isocrates VIII 82 it is inferred that delegations bringing the tribute to Athens were sent by the tribute-paying states to arrive at the time of the City Dionysia. The Lenaea (at which *Acharnians* was produced) was a winter festival and did not coincide with numerous foreigners being at Athens. Thus Aristophanes says that there are no foreigners present, only citizens; 'grain but no chaff'. Resident foreigners (cf. l. 508) are the bran. They had their freedom but could not qualify for citizenship mererly by the length of their stay at Athens, since this depended on parentage, or (which was very rare) a decision of the assembly.

I hope Poseidon sends an earthquake: Poseidon was the god both of the sea and of earthquakes, which were believed to be caused by the movement of underground rivers. Just such an earthquake as that for which Dikaiopolis here prays devastated Sparta in 464 BC and resulted in a helot uprising. The cause of the incident had then been attributed to divine displeasure, because the Spartans had put to death a number of helots in the sanctuary of Poseidon on Cape Taenarum (Thuc. I 218.1).

p. 72   **Athenians...started the whole thing**: Relations between Athens and Megara had for a long time been strained. Megara bordered Attica to the West. In 433 BC the Megarians complained to the Spartans that they had been unlawfully banned from Athenian markets (Thuc. I 67.4). The Spartans demanded that the Athenians retract the decree which had secured this exclusion of the Megarians, but without success. The Athenians claimed that their actions were justified because the Megarians had infringed their borders (Thuc. I 139.2). Plutarch, probably following Aristophanes, names Pericles as the originator of the decree; Thucydides does not name a proposer for the decree.

Started bringing charges against the Megarians: The word used for 'to bring charges against' is deliberately chosen, being *sukophantein*. Those who manipulated the judicial system at Athens for their own gain were known as *sukophantai*.

'Megarian contraband': Import dues were levied upon goods crossing the borders into Attica. Avoidance of these was no doubt commonplace and must often have led to friction between two countries. The sale of confiscated goods helped to recompense the state treasury for lost revenue.

Simaetha: She is not known and is not necessarily a real person.

Aspasia: She was the mistress of Pericles (Plutarch *Pericles* 24.3) and naturally offered the comic poets a tempting target for scurrilous attacks upon Pericles himself (cf. Cratinus frag. 241), one such being the allegation that she influenced him to start the Peloponnesian War.

The cause of the war: Satiric half truths masquerading as facts both amuse and entertain, but the causes of the war here quoted cannot realistically be given credence (a quite different account of the reasons for the Megarian Decree is given in *Peace*). Thucydides gives yet another assessment of the outbreak of hostilities (I 23 and I 66). He alone of the ancient sources seems to play down the Megarian Decree, deliberately concentrating on the Corinthian grievances.

Olympian Pericles: The comic poets and especially Cratinus gave Pericles this title in view of the length of his ascendancy at Athens, his dignity and aloofness.

'No Megarian shall stand on sea or on land...': The Megarian Decree (cf. Thuc. I 67.4) did indeed exclude the Megarians from 'the harbours of the Athenian Empire and the Attic market' (Thuc. I 139). The significance of the Decree to the outbreak of the war may be seen from Thucydides' account. Initially the Spartans had demanded that the Megarian Decree be revoked, that the siege of Potidaea be abandoned and that Aegina be granted independence. The most important issue would appear to have been the Decree. The Athenians refused to comply, accusing Megara of having cultivated consecrated land belonging to them. The final Spartan ultimatum declared that Sparta wanted peace and that this was still possible if the Athenians gave the Hellenes their freedom. Again the matter was discussed at Athens and significantly the Megarian Decree seems to have been the central issue. 'Many speakers came forward and opinions were expressed on either side, some maintaining that war was necessary and others saying that the Megarian Decree should be revoked and not allowed to stand in the way of peace'. Among those who spoke against revoking the decree was Pericles, who made a point of stressing the importance of 'the small matter proving the Athenians determination'.

I hear someone say that they ought not to have declared war: This is once again a quotation from *Telephus*, as also are lines 543 and 555.

Seriphos: This island, which lay in the Cyclades group of the Western Aegean, is chosen for its insignificance. An interesting light seems to be shed on the Athenians' attitude to the Megarians by this comparison.

p. 73   **The City would have been full of military preparations**: We are treated to a surprisingly detailed description of the preparations for war, including the minutiae of men partying before an expedition. Even if this is not the material of an historical text book it does help to give an intimate picture of the people.

Figure-heads of Athena being gilded: The image of Athena was in fact placed upon the stern of the boat.

Dikaiopolis' argument wins the support of half the chorus. The remainder, threatened by this attack upon their resolve for war, call upon their champion, Lamachus. Dikaiopolis mocks Lamachus by feigning fear, by making coarse insinuations and by implying that the general has dishonest motives. The lampoon is hardly justified but the comic discomfiture of a representative of the war faction is successful in winning over the chorus.

p. 74   **Lamachus**: Aristophanes' caricature of him casts him as a bellicose but misguided warrior who seeks personal financial gain from the war (cf. ll. 597 ff., p. 75). We have no reason to consider this view justified. In fact in his later plays after Lamachus' death Aristophanes pays tribute to his bravery (*Thesm.*, l. 841; *Frogs*, l. 1039).

Lord of the Gorgon Crest: The chorus call upon Lamachus as if he were a deity ('come quickly' is commonly used in prayer to a god). The address 'Lord of the Gorgon Crest' refers both to a magnificent plume of feathers on his helmet and to a gorgon motif upon his shield.

Who has aroused the Gorgon on my targe?: Lamachus speaks as if the shield had an identity of its own.

O Lord Feathercrest: Dikaiopolis sarcastically belittles the crest.

Please take away that bugaboo: Dikaiopolis is again being sarcastic, pretending to be afraid. He uses a word associated with children's stories of monsters.

p. 75   **A boastard**: Dikaiopolis invents a bird's name to poke further fun at the mighty warrior. The *kompolakuthos* is a bird whose name suggests 'boastful talk' (*kompolakein*).

Trim my wick...you're well enough equipped to do it!: Dikaiopolis enrages the great man by this double entendre. Respectfully he might be saying 'you are well enough equipped with weapons to cut me to pieces'. Dikaiopolis' actions if not his words will have made clear his other meaning, for he may well have offered the phallus which he wore to be circumcised, or as Dover suggests (*Greek Homosexuality*, p. 204) have displayed his anus and gesticulated with his penis in a mock enactment of the homosexual act. Lamachus is 'well enough equipped' because of the size of his penis which he is invited to use, while at the same time giving Dikaiopolis stimulation by 'trimming his wick'. In either case Dikaiopolis both acts submissively and subtly continues to tease his adversary.

In the pay queue: Pay (*misthos*) had by this time been introduced for most offices at Athens. Since it provided a recompense for lost earnings it enabled many citizens to participate in political decision-making. The Athenians were justifiably proud of this, but even they realised that the system was open to abuse as this and the following lines suggest. There would also have been those who would prefer to keep political office to the rich.

As far away from the scene of the action as you possibly could: An accusation made earlier in the play, that money and people are being wastefully employed on embassies to far off places without due attention being focused upon the war with Sparta, is again repeated in the following lines. At the heart of the play we find the incisiveness of the layman's view, despite its naivety, challenging the supposed wisdom of the duly elected expert.

To Thrace, perhaps, on three drachmas a day: Thrace was to the north of Greece. Chaonia was a tribal state of Epirus in much the same area as modern Albania. Northern Greece was an important source of wood and minerals, and alliances were sought there by both the Athenians and the Spartans.

p. 76   **Camarina, Gela, Catana, Ridicula**: Since both Athens and Sparta had allies in Sicily, the Sicilians became involved in the Peloponnesian war. Camarina, Gela and Catana are Sicilian towns. Since Gela suggests the Greek word *gelos* meaning 'laughter', Aristophanes punningly follows this with the imaginary Sicilian city named *katagelos*, meaning 'ridicule'.

Marilades....: Each of the names is fictitious. Marilades (son of coal-dust), Anthracyllus (little charcoal), Euphorides (good lifter), Prinides (oakman).

Ecbatana: Cf. note p. 52.

Coesyra's son: Coesyra was proverbially the name given to any rich and proud woman (cf. *Clouds*, pp. 114 and 145). The scholia identify the son as Megacles, probably the son of Megacles of the Alkmaeonid family (cf. *Clouds*, note p. 114).

Club subscriptions: Associations were formed to aid indebted friends. The subscription to these provided an insurance policy for the individual should hard times occur.

Oh, Democracy!: Like Poseidon in *Birds*, ll. 1570 f., Lamachus exclaims thus, finding the system intolerable which encourages his inferiors to aspire to high office and to insult people like him.

The departure of Lamachus and then Dikaiopolis, together with the aptly worded stage direction of Sommerstein ('looking after the departing "hero"') leaves us with the important question: 'Who is the hero of the play?' Lamachus is in a sense 'heroic'; the supporter of the democracy and the fearless warrior. Dikaiopolis by comparison is the weakling. Neither, however, can be taken entirely seriously, since the one is clearly far larger than life and the other, despite the attractions of the escapism which he offers, is an equally unreal character whose ideas are largely wishful thinking.

In the Parabasis (ll. 626-718, pp. 77-81) the chorus leader takes up the cause of the city's older people, which was begun by Dikaiopolis in his accusations against Lamachus. They, he says, had bravely defended the city in the past but now find themselves dragged into court by younger men who are ambitious for success. The lawcourts (*dikasteria*) not only decided criminal charges and disputes between individuals but also acted to protect the constitution by examining state officials. This system, particularly in political matters, was open to abuse (see below, note p. 79).

p. 77   **Let's strip for the dance**: Physical exercise, as in the gymnasium, was generally taken naked. Here the chorus simply remove their cloaks so that they may be unhindered as they dance.

Our poet: The Greek word translated 'our poet' in this line is *didaskalos*, which in a theatrical context means 'producer'. The word more commonly translating 'poet' (*poietes*) is used at line 645. Records show that Aristophanes' first three plays were produced by a man called Callistratos. Since the terms for producer and poet are interchanged it is not clear to whom these lines refer.

But since his foes have charged him: Once again the reference is to Cleon's prosecution of Aristophanes in the previous year (cf. note p. 66).

'Violet-crowned': The praise is that of the poet Pindar, as is 'rich and shining'.

Exactly what 'democracy' means to a subject state: Without *Babylonians* we cannot be sure what is meant by this. Perhaps Aristophanes had there sought to express the allied view of the Athenian democracy, not least the 'meddlesomeness' (*polupragmosune*), as Thucydides termed it, of the Athenians and in particular of her officials and administrators posted in the allied states. Cleon and his adherents were particularly responsible for the tightening of Athenian control over her subjects.

p. 78   **When the Spartans sent their envoys to the Persian court**: The Spartans had sent an embassy to Persia at the beginning of the war (Thuc. II 7) and again in 425 BC (Thuc. VI 50). It was believed that Persian financial and especially naval support would break the deadlock of the war. The Spartans had traditionally been the leading Greek state because of their military prestige, but although they could at will overrun most of Attica, they could not inflict a decisive defeat upon a sea-power.

That comic poet, what's-his-name: There is a sudden transition from serious to comic comment. But even here there is room for a serious point; that the comic poet can be an effective teacher.

Peace proposals made by Sparta: According to an earlier treaty made between Athens and Sparta in 445 BC (Thuc. I 67) Aegina was to be guaranteed her independence. The Aeginetans complained to the Spartans that this had not been granted, occasioning one of the Spartan demands at the outbreak of the war in 431 BC (cf. Thuc. I 139). Shortly after the beginning of the war the Athenians drove out the island's inhabitants and planted their own settlers there. Peace proposals were made by the Spartans in 430 BC but Thucydides makes no mention of Aegina in connection with these (cf. Thuc. II 59.2 and II 65.2).

To take away our poet: It is supposed from this that Aristophanes had some connection with Aegina; perhaps of family or of land in consequence of the expulsions of 430 BC.

p. 79   **Come hither, glowing charcoal Muse**: Appropriately the chorus of Acharnians make their invocation to a 'charcoal Muse' (cf. note p. 63). At *Lys.* l. 1297 a Muse similarly befitting the chorus is addressed.

The bright-crowned Thasian sauce: Sprats dipped in sauce were a speciality of the island of Thasos (cf. *Wasps*, ll. 329-31). 'Bright-crowned', comically describing the sauce as if it were a person, is explained by commentators as referring to the shining oil that rises to the surface.

The young accuser, scorning others' aid: Indictments were brought by private individuals whether they involved a personal dispute or an offence against the state. Some aspiring young speakers carved out political careers for themselves by bringing the latter type of accusation. On certain rare occasions the state appointed prosecutors called *sunegoroi* (the word translated by 'accuser' here). Such appointments were sought by those anxious for advancement.

p. 80   **Marathon**: In 490 BC the Athenians defeated the invading Persian host at Marathon in the North-east of Attica. Some support was given by the Plataeans but it was a source of pride that the victory was gained almost single-handed. The chorus claim that they deserve better treatment since they fought bravely for their country at Marathon (cf. p. 57 and note).

Pursued: There is a play on the double meaning of the Greek word *diokein* here. It can mean 'pursue' or 'prosecute'. In fact our English words are in origin identical, and in Scottish 'the pursuer' can still be used of 'the prosecutor'. It is followed in the next line by a word meaning both 'be captured' and 'be convicted', which is translated for us as, 'And we're persecuted, we for mercy plead'. The word-play neatly links the transition from fighting at Marathon to contesting in court.

Thucydides: Thucydides, the son of Melesias (not the historian), in the 440's organized and led the opposition to Pericles. In 443 BC he was ostracised from Athens for ten years, after which time he returned and once again tried to exert his influence in politics against Pericles. His old age apparently left him bereft of the oratorical skills he had once possessed, since while facing accusations brought by Cephisodemus in 426/5 BC he broke down and was unable to make his defence.

Lost in the Scythian wilderness: Scythia, the Southern steppes of Russia, was in Greek minds a vast tract of land inhabited by barbarians. Thucydides would seem in other words to be completely at sea. However, the structure of the Greek makes it possible to read 'Scythian wilderness' as if it were a person with whom Thucydides fought and lost. 'Wilderness' is thus being figuratively used of a barren and savage man, and refers to Cephisodemus.

That taunting scion of the archer race: The Scythians were famous as bowmen. At Athens the name 'Scythian archer' was given to the slaves who policed the city. As in line 704 above this is a denigration of Cephisodemus' birth with possibly an added insinuation about his status.

He'd not have stood such insults from Demeter!: The reference to Demeter, the goddess of the harvest, makes no sense and may be the result of an incorrect manuscript reading. The meaning is presumably that Thucydides in his prime was unbeatable by anyone.

He'd have floored them all: The metaphor is appropriately used of Thucydides, whose father was a trainer of wrestlers.

p. 81   **Queers like Alcibiades**: At the time of this play he was about twenty-five years old but had already made a name for himself. He was ambitious, wealthy and often unscrupulous. His lifestyle was extravagant, his behaviour promiscuous. His lovers were of both sexes.

'The young should fight the young, the old the old': Aristophanes remodels a proverb ('knock out a nail with a nail') for this concluding line. Aristophanes frequently dramatizes the conflict of young and old in his plays.

Now that he has secured his own peace, Dikaiopolis establishes his own market from which none, except Lamachus, are excluded. In the scenes that follow we see some of the transactions of this 'open' market and the opposition that it faces. The first to arrive is an impoverished and starving Megarian who sells his daughters in order to obtain food. His plight is not an occasion for a humanitarian plea for peace but for a bawdy scene in which the Megarian dialect is mimicked.

p. 82 **Market Commissioners:** There were ten such officials (*agoranomoi*) at Athens. They oversaw the smooth running of the agora and enforced any laws relating to it. Dikaiopolis appoints for himself three leather whips to keep order in his market place.

Lepri: Some have suggested that this was a place near Athens which had a tannery, but there is no evidence for this. Others see a pun upon *lepein* 'to skin', appropriately used of a whip.

Informers: Cf. note p. 72.

Or any other bird of that feather: *Phasianos* in Greek is a 'pheasant'. The word is used here to refer to an informer because of a pun on the word *phasis* which is a 'denunciation'. Similar puns are found on pp. 87 and 90.

Go and get my engraved copy of the peace treaty: Important official decrees were recorded upon stone. In 421 BC the terms of the Peace of Nicias were set up on pillars at various important centres (Thuc. V 18.10).

Megarian: The poor Megarian who now appears with his starving daughters speaks in his own Doric dialect.

The great god of friendship: This is a title given to Zeus.

p. 83 **A guid Megarian trick:** Megarians seem to have been associated with coarseness, vulgarity and treachery. This is also the implication of *Wasps*, l. 57. The nature of the trick about to be played here fits with this, and the audience perhaps, well aware of the reputation that the Megarians had, have their appetites whetted.

Canties – is it piglets they ca' them?: After the more subtle double-entendres we have already met, which would have required an attentive theatre-goer, the pun upon the meaning of *khoiros* being either a 'pig' (a common enough Megarian export, cf. l. 521, p. 72) or 'vulva' is crude and laboured.

For Hermes knows: He was the god of journeys and travelling, as well as being the messenger of the gods.

The Mysteries doon at Eleusis: At Eleusis on the coast west of Athens secret rites were celebrated in honour of Demeter. Initiates probably underwent a symbolic death to be reborn into a new life. As a preliminary they sacrificed a young pig (cf. *Frogs*, l. 338).

We sit by the fire and shrink: The Megarian says that he and his companions sit by the fire 'starving competitively' (*diapeinames*); in other words arguing about who is the more hungry. Dikaiopolis speaks as if he mishears and thinks that they sit by the fire 'drinking' (*diapinomes*).

Then you'll be out of the wood before long: To the sarcasm of the previous line Dikaiopolis adds this touch of black humour. Their escape will be in death.

It's sae high, the gods in heaven are takkin' it a'!: The Greek word usually applied to the gods meaning 'highly honoured' is here used to mean 'very expensive'.

p. 84   **Din ye own the whole of the sea already?**: The Athenians with their huge navy were able to control the seas around Greece, but the reference is probably more specific. In 427 BC the Athenians captured the island of Minoa off the Megarian coast and were able from here to obstruct Megarian salt workings.

Every time ye raid our country: Before and after the Spartan invasions of Attica the Athenians would attack the Megarid.

This is a proper pure-bred Greek cantie: The anticipated moment is at hand when the true nature of the Megarian's produce is revealed.

p. 85   **Where's its tail...it'll have a beautiful fat red one**: Dikaiopolis suggests that the pig is imperfect and therefore unsuitable for purchase and for sacrifice. The Megarian, who is thinking on different terms from those of Dikaiopolis, replies that it will 'have' or rather will 'accommodate' a tail/penis in due course.

But you don't sacrifice these to Aphrodite: Dikaiopolis gives a further reason for not wanting the pigs. Since Aphrodite's lover Adonis had been killed by a boar, the goddess was worshipped without the sacrificial slaughter of pigs. The Megarian counters by suggesting that a *khoiros* in its other sense is a most appropriate offering to the goddess of sexual love.

If you stick them on a spit: The double meaning needs no explanation.

p. 86   **Phibalian figs**: A Phibalian was a kind of fig tree. The scholiast says that the word was applied figuratively to lean, leathery people.

Mighty Heracles: Heracles, the glutton, is appropriately invoked here.

A bunch of garlic...four poond o' salt: In exchange for his daughters the Megarian asks for comparatively small quantities of the very commodities his country had once produced in abundance.

In that case I denounce these piglets: The informer could benefit by up to half the value of the property confiscated.

p. 87 **I'm being informerized**: The Megarian's attempt at the correct Attic legal terminology is comical. He coins a new use of *phantazomai*, related to the word *phaino* 'inform' (cf. note p. 82), by using it incorrectly to mean 'be informed (against)'.

What do you think you are charging people like this...?: The double sense in which 'charge' is used mirrors a similar expression in the Greek again involving the word *phaino*.

Dikaiopolis is congratulated by the chorus because, in establishing his own market, he has escaped the worst clientele of the Agora. This provides the occasion for a vitriolic attack upon the more infamous of those who frequented the Agora. Although short, this passage gives an idea of the bustle of the Athenian market-place and of its most colourful characters. We are reminded in particular that it was far more than a market-place. It was an administrative and religious centre for the city, where many met to barter, trade, seek information or advice, pay respect to the gods, or simply to talk.

After the Megarian a Boeotian comes to Dikaiopolis' market with fowls for sale. Again an opportunity to mimic dialect is not missed. The Boeotian is not sure what he wants from the Attic market. Dikaiopolis has the bright idea of selling him a commodity that is in plentiful supply at Athens, an informer.

Ctesias: We assume from this passage that he could be regarded as an informer, but otherwise nothing is known of him.

p. 88 **Cleonymus**: Cf. note p. 53.

Hyperbolus: After the death of Cleon in 422 BC he succeeded him in the assembly and in the comic poets' scorn. He appears to have owed his success, at least in part, to his activity in the courts, for which he became proverbial (cf. 'more litigious than Hyperbolus'). In 416 BC he was ostracised and in 411 BC he was murdered during an oligarchic coup.

Cratinus: Cratinus the comic poet is probably meant, although the scholiast thinks otherwise suggesting the reference is to an unknown lyric poet. Together with Aristophanes and Eupolis he was later considered one of the three great exponents of Old Comedy. He had a reputation for drunkenness, a fact which he himself parodied in one of his plays, as well as for an unkempt appearance and an excessive exuberance for writing, and it would seem talking (cf.

Athenaeus 39c; *Knights*, ll. 531-4 and 526 ff.; and l. 1173, p. 102 below).

Lysistratus: He is mentioned elsewhere by Aristophanes (cf. *Wasps*, ll. 787-95 and 1308-13), where he appears to be a practical joker.

BOEOTIAN: Boeotia, a federation of states dominated by Thebes, lay to the north of Attica. Aristophanes mimics the Boeotian dialect as he had the Megarian. This new character with his fowls for sale is very different from the last visitor to Dikaiopolis' market. A far more cheerful character than the Megarian, he comes with his troop of pipers. He has not known the deprivations of the former and cannot as easily be tempted by the items for sale in the Athenian market.

Boi Heracles: Thebes, the most powerful city in Boeotia, was the birthplace of Heracles and therefore the oath is appropriately made.

'The Dog's Arse': Some suggest that this is a crude reference to a form of bag-pipes, others that it is to a well-known tune.

Chaeris: Cf. p. 49.

Boi Iolaus: This time the oath is sworn by Iolaus, the friend of Heracles.

p. 89 **I can see you've brought fowl weather!:** The north wind forced birds southwards and therefore was sometimes referred to as 'bird bearing'. This as applied to the Boeotian is particularly apt, since he carries in his sack fowls which he wants to sell.

Some eels from Lake Copais: These were a great delicacy (cf. *Lys.*, ll. 36 and 702, pp. 181 and 209, and *Wasps*, l. 510).

Man's highest joy: The rapture of Dikaiopolis' welcome for the eels is a parody of the conventional reunion scene of tragedy. Aristophanes may have had one or more plays specifically in mind but these cannot be identified with certainty, except in lines 883 and 893-4.

O eldest of the daughters of Copais: This is a parody of a line from Aeschylus (frag. 174).

How joyful will the chorus members be: This breaks the dramatic illusion (cf. notes pp. 68 and 69). The chorus will be well pleased if, after the performance, they are feasted on eels. The chorus director was expected to provide for the party that followed the production (cf. ll. 1150-5, p. 101; also *Clouds*, ll. 338-9, p. 126).

For nor alive nor dead would I be parted from my well-loved eel: These are the words of Admetus (apart from the 'well loved eel') to his dying wife, Alcestis, in the Euripidean play of that name (367-8).

p. 90 **Market dues:** Foreigners importing and selling goods in the Athenian market were taxed. The same applies in Dikaiopolis' market.

Phalerum whitebait: Phalerum was the wide bay to the east of Piraeus.

I'm still quite in the dark: The translation expands and makes more explicit the pun upon the two senses of *phaino* meaning 'make clear' and 'lay information about...' (cf. l. 826, p. 86). The Greek word *dia* in this sentence can also be used to suggest different interpretations. Either the charge is brought 'because of' the lamp-wicks, or it is 'by their means' that the issue is clarified.

The Docks: Since Athenian strength depended upon her navy, fear that an enemy might set fire to their ships in the dock was no doubt always present.

To light up shady deeds: Once again *phaino* is used with two meanings (cf. ll. 823 and 917, pp. 86 and 90). The Greek is more specific about the 'shady deeds', refering to the annual check upon outgoing officials. The lantern will be used to 'expose' (corruption).

The Boeotian and his slave leave carrying their burden. At this moment a slave arrives from Lamachus who wishes to make purchases on behalf of his master. We now see how Lamachus and Dikaiopolis have fared since their earlier confrontation. Lamachus is suffering from the war-economy, but Dikaiopolis has peace and plenty. This point is further emphasized as various individuals intrude lamenting their losses and seeking help. Finally a messenger arrives to summon Lamachus to war; a second invites Dikaiopolis to a feast. As Lamachus prepares, Dikaiopolis apes his words and his manner.

The Festival of Pitchers: This was part of the festival of the Anthesteria which was held in early spring (February). During the celebrations of the Anthesteria the new wine was blessed and enjoyed by all, including the children, who came carrying their drinking jugs. For further details cf. H.W. Parke *Festivals of the Athenians* (London, 1977) pp. 107-20.

A drachma...and three: Since a drachma was at least equivalent to a day's wage, these seem to be high prices to pay even for luxury items.

Three mighty crests: Tydeus is said by Aeschylus to wear three crests (*Seven Against Thebes*, l. 384). The ridicule of this reference may be twofold if, as there is reason to think (cf. Sommerstein *CQ* 28 [1978] p. 383), the name of Lamachus' son was Tydeus. Firstly, Lamachus is mocked for his vain desire to fight as Tydeus; secondly, for his fanatical obsession with war in naming his son after the epic hero.

He's got some salt fish already: These were probably included in the soldier's rations. They were cheap and despised. Dikaiopolis impertinently tells Lamachus to go and frighten someone else with his mighty crests so that they give him something to eat. Alternatively he may be fancifully suggesting that Lamachus' threatening plumes might be used to season the unpalatable dish.

Dikaiopolis goes into his house and the chorus move forward to address the audience (in the Second Parabasis, ll. 971-99, pp. 94-5). They emphasize the benefits of peace which Dikaiopolis now enjoys, and contrast these with the disadvantages of war. War is a gate-crasher of the party at which the peace-time delicacies are enjoyed. The drunken, violent War destroys the fun. Finally, when the audience have taken in this image of War, they are presented with the fact that he not only ruins the party but also the vines which produce the wine for the party.

p. 94 **The cup of friendship**: As an act of friendship two parties would each drink to the other's health from the same cup (cf. *Lys.*, l. 203, p. 187 and ll. 238-9, p. 189).

See the tokens of rejoicing lie before our hero's door!: These tokens are feathers dropped by Dikaiopolis as he struggled into the house with the birds he had purchased from the Boeotian. They may be contrasted with the spoils of war which would more usually be made to adorn doorposts (cf. note p. 98 'Who is it knocks without these brazen halls?').

Reconciliation: To contrast the rowdy and drunken personification of War in the previous stanza, the chorus imagine Reconciliation as a beautiful maiden (cf. *Lys.*, ll. 1114 ff., p. 226).

Cytherean graces: The goddess Aphrodite was said to have emerged from the sea (as from the womb) on Cyprus, but she had first passed near the island of Cythera. The myth is an attempt to explain her name and cult titles (Cyprogenes, Cythereia; cf. Hesiod *Theogony*, l. 192).

As in Zeuxis' picture: According to the scholia a picture of Eros 'adorned with roses' was to be found in the temple of Aphrodite at Athens.

p. 95 **First I'd plant a few young fig-trees**: Once again we witness the longing of the Attic farmer for peace and a return to his fields. However, the continuity of the lines cannot be fully understood unless their double meaning is appreciated. The chorus leader's thoughts have turned to love and in particular to sexual fulfilment. He may be old but he fancies the idea of being reconciled with Reconciliation.

He thinks he might be able to do so three times! Agricultural terms were commonly used in Greek of sexual activity, hence here 'plant', 'a circle/enclosure' (cf. 'vale' used of the female genitals at *Lys.*, l. 88, p. 183).

You and I could be anointed: This is done in preparation for a feast, but sexual innuendo is also present (cf. *Lys.*, ll. 940 ff., p. 219 'Take this bottle...').

Win a skinful of Ctesiphon: The prizes for drinking contests such as those held at the Anthesteria would usually be a skinful of wine (cf. l. 1225, p. 104). Ctesiphon, who is otherwise unknown, was presumably a fat man, perhaps reputed for his consumption of alcohol. To receive a skinful of Ctesiphon would be little different from winning a wineskin; one's reward would be to acquire a belly not unlike his.

p. 96   **Please give me a little**: The play upon the double meaning of the word *sponde* used at ll. 178 ff., p. 57 (cf. 'These three peaces') is repeated here. It is further developed in the last scenes.

I live at Phyle: Phyle was a deme of Attica situated in the mountainous region bordering Boeotia to the north. It was particularly hard pressed by enemy raids.

The source of all the good manure I ever got: The alteration of a single word, 'manure' for 'blessings', gives a surprising twist to a common phrase.

The state physician: According to Plato some doctors were employed by the state to give free treatment to all citizens (*Gorgias* 455B and 514D-515B). Since Dikaiopolis has won for himself a private peace he argues that he is under no such obligation as the state physicians to share it.

p. 97   **In this bottle**: For the sexual innuendo of this request cf. note to *Lys.*, ll. 947-8, p. 219.

Let's hear what she has to say: The whispered message and the ensuing sniggers are often used in comedy to increase speculation about the nature of the secret communication.

pp. 97-8   **She is a woman, and it would be wrong for her to suffer by the war**: Women did not have a vote and were therefore not connected with political decision making. Since she does not deserve to suffer from the war for which she is not responsible, Dikaiopolis will give her the help for which she asks.

p. 98   **Just smear a little of this on to his prick at night**: We may compare the witchcraft of Simaetha who in Theocritus (*Idylls* II) uses charms and potions similarly at night to attempt to win back her lover.

Bringing bad news, by the look of his face: Actors wore masks with exaggerated features. This sort of introduction for a newcomer to the scene is common in tragedy, especially where a messenger enters to report important events (cf. Euripides' *Hippolytus*, l. 1152).

O War! O Ares! O Lamachus!: The pun of line 270 (cf. note p. 61) is repeated.

Who is it knocks without these brazen halls?: Lamachus appears from his house. His speech, as earlier, is more akin to that of tragedy, making him sound grandiose and pompous. We may imagine that the house is secured and adorned from top to bottom with military weaponry and regalia. The house is as excessive as its dweller is obsessive.

In the snow: The Festival of the Anthesteria was celebrated in February when snow normally falls in the mountains between Attica and Boeotia.

Like to have a fight with Geryon, Heracles?: In the tenth of his labours Heracles slew Geryon, a monster with three heads and bodies (Hesiod *Theogony*, l. 287; Euripides *Heracles*, l. 423). As Lamachus turns and threatens Dikaiopolis, the latter adopts a tauntingly submissive pose. The translation and the stage directions suggest that Dikaiopolis pretends to be a locust, but it is not clear why he should do this except that his reference to four wings may imply that he assumes the posture of an insect, perhaps flat on the floor or pretending to fly away. Nevertheless this interpretation seems unsatisfactory. A slight change in one word would give the sense '[as] Geryon against a locust' or another slight change '[as] a locust against Geryon'. Possibly a proverbial expression underlies one or other of these.

The Priest of Dionysus: He would have organized and overseen the Festival of the Anthesteria. Since theatrical performances were celebrated in honour of the same god, the priest of Dionysus would also have attended on this occasion, sitting in the front row watching the play (cf. *Frogs*, l. 297).

p. 99   **You chose to enlist under the Gorgon:**. Lamachus has the Gorgon's head emblazoned on his shield. He has, says Dikaiopolis, chosen to follow the way of war with this monster as his guardian spirit, and should therefore not now complain of its hardships.

My provision basket: This is to be compared with the boxful of meat which Dikaiopolis carries (cf. l. 1086, 'my dinner box' and note p. 103) and is the first of many such comparisons.

p. 100   **Locusts**: Dikaiopolis imagines that Lamachus may be forced to eat locusts through lack of provisions.

The stand for my shield: A small easel was used to support the shield for display purposes. Dikaiopolis, by comparing the rounded shield to his belly (indeed the former may have provided a slang word for the latter), calls for loaves of bread to sustain him.

Absolutely disgusting!: The Greek has 'flatly disgusting' to contrast with the jokes that have previously involved comparisons of rounded objects.

p. 101　　**The son of – of Gorgonus**: With mock fear Dikaiopolis taunts Lamachus whom he addresses as 'the son of Gorgonus'. This invented patronymic refers to the Gorgon motif on the hero's shield (for similar inventions cf. note p. 54 'Cleisthenes' and note p. 101 'Antimachus') as well as to his ferocious character.

This will defend me stoutly: The verb used here is equally applicable to fitting on armour and to taking a stiff drink.

Antimachus: From the present context we learn that Antimachus was nick-named 'Splutterer'. He is here accused of having failed to perform the duties of a *choregos* because of his meanness. He was expected to provide a meal for the chorus after the performance. The implication of what is said here is that either he did not provide such a meal or that what he did provide was not worth having. Since the position of *choregos* was one which was undertaken by the rich as a form of taxation but also as a means of winning esteem the accusation is doubly damning.

p. 102　　**Just as it's lying waiting safe and sound**: The key word in this and the following lines is *paralos*, which usually means 'beside the sea'. The cuttlefish would then be freshly cooked on the seashore. But 'the Paralos' was also a messenger ship of the Athenian navy and therefore a pun is developed in the succeeding lines in which the tray of sizzling cuttlefish is said to capsize and run aground.

Cratinus: Cf. note p. 88.

A messenger suddenly enters, bringing news that Lamachus has been wounded. The stricken hero soon follows, bewailing his misfortune. Next Dikaiopolis arrives, probably from the other side of the stage. He is staggering and suffering the consequences of his drinking. Lamachus speaks as if he were uttering a tragic dirge. Dikaiopolis' speech, which mirrors this, contrasts the anguish of battle and proclaims the joys of peace. Dikaiopolis is quick to seize upon and exploit the words of Lamachus, who in his agony is unaware of the interjections.

The translator omits eight lines (ll. 1182-9) which are now

considered genuine. They are seemingly nonsensical and therefore some have suggested that they have been interpolated. But such messenger speeches before the *exodos* of the play are also found in *Birds* (ll. 1706-19) and *Eccl.* (ll. 1112-26) which are similarly difficult to understand. The fact that tragic diction is here (and in *Birds*) being mimicked might account for their incoherence. The speaker in *Eccl.* is drunk. Furthermore, the scholiast says that l. 1188 is taken from Euripides' *Telephus* which tends to validate it and the preceding lines. For a fuller discussion cf. Sommerstein *CQ* (1978) pp. 390-5.

p. 103   **Who ever heard of charging for anything on Pitcher Day?**: Dikaiopolis mocks Lamachus by taking the word 'charge' in a different sense. On the feast day contributions to food were expected (cf. l. 1086, p. 99), but no money would have changed hands.

Save me, great Apollo!: The phraseology of the line is typically tragic. Apollo, the god of healing, is appropriately invoked.

It's not his feast today: It was the feast of Dionysus, whether that be at the Lenaia or at the Anthesteria.

How dizzy is my head...and says it's time for bed: Aristophanes coins the word *skotobinio* 'feel faint through desire of making love' to correspond to *skotodinio* meaning 'feel dizzy'.

p. 104   **Where are you, judges? Where's the King?**: Dikaiopolis is claiming his prize from the judges of the drinking competition and hopes to receive this from the King (*Basileus*) Archon who presided at the festivities. The *Basileus* Archon was appointed annually by lot and was responsible primarily for religious matters, among which were the supervision of the Pitcher Festival (cf. note l. 961, p. 93) as well as the Lenaia. As Aristophanes brings his play to a conclusion he makes an appeal, although diguised, to the judges of the dramatic competition and to the King Archon sitting in the front row of the audience. Such a direct appeal was not uncommon (cf. *Clouds*, l. 1115, p. 158; *Birds*, l. 1101 and *Eccl.*, l. 1154).

'Hail to the champion': Thus began an ode of Archilochus to Heracles. It became a common salute for any victor but particularly those who had won Olympic victories.

Lysistrata

At the beginning of the play Lysistrata stands in front of the Propylaea awaiting the arrival of the women she has summoned to an important meeting. During the *prologos* she tells her friend Calonice of her plan to save Greece from war. Her idea is to hold a sex strike. The curiosity of the spectators is aroused by the gradual revelation of the plan. When the women from Sparta, Thebes and Corinth do arrive, they are not easily convinced about this scheme, but Lysistrata is supported by her Spartan counterpart, Lampito. After the women have sworn an oath that they will abstain from sexual intercourse, they each go back to their respective countries.

p. 180 **Bacchic celebration**: Bacchus or Dionysus, being the god of wine, presided over many festivities and celebrations, among which were the theatrical contests where tragic and comic plays were produced. He was also a divinity in whose rites women played a prominent part (cf. Euripides' *Bacchae*).

Pan or Aphrodite: Pan was a native god of Arcadia whose chief function concerned the fertility of the flocks. He was therefore often portrayed as being amorous, a quality he shares with Aphrodite. She was the Greek goddess of beauty, love and fertility. In literature she is particularly associated with sexual desire. Interestingly, in antiquity it appears to have been the women who had the 'one track minds'. Perhaps it would be fairer to say that the insatiability of women appealed to the sexist attitudes of the predominantly male audience.

We're such clever villains: That women were scheming and mischievous is common in myth and tragedy (cf. Phaedra, Medea, Helen). It is particularly associated with Euripidean heroines, but goes back at least to Hesiod's myth of Pandora. Aristophanes exploits this villainous characterization of women also in *Thesm.* (where they plot to kill Euripides) and in *Eccl.* (where they plot to take over the assembly).

pp. 180-1 **It's not so easy for a wife**: One wonders whether the description of a woman's lot in the lines that follow are any less a stereotype than the mockery of their sexual urges above.

p. 181   **Is it something big?**: A favourite device of comedy is to have two people talking at cross purposes where sexual innuendoes are obvious (cf. *Ach.*, p. 85). As often in Aristophanic comedy the joke is maintained for several lines, hence 'thick', 'flimsy' and 'tossing to and fro'.

We might as well give up hope, then: The Greek word *lepton* 'flimsy' is often proverbially used in expressions of hope.

Do spare the eels: Boeotia bordered Attica to the North. The eels imported from here were in peace time a great delicacy at Athens (cf. *Ach.*, p. 89).

Well, I won't say it...: To the Greek it was the verbal expression, not the thought, that was ill-omened. Lysistrata will not say that the Athenians may be defeated.

Putting on cosmetics and saffron gowns: Clothes that were dyed with the costly yellow dye were kept for special, often ceremonial, occasions (cf. p. 207 and note 'To Brauron town'). At *Clouds*, l. 51, p. 114, the putting on of saffron dyed garments is, as here, associated with sensuality.

p. 182   **I'm going to get some new dye...**: Calonice is willing to take part in a scheme that will bring an end to the war, if all that means is dressing attractively. She may also be looking forward to having her husband home from war and in her bed. She is less ready to deny herself when she realizes what Lysistrata is asking of her (cf. p. 185).

They ought to have taken wing and flown here: If it is the return of their men that is at stake, then, thinks Calonice, the other women should be here now.

They're Athenian and do everything too late: This was a common enough complaint from the orators of the next century (cf. Demosthenes *First Philippic* 49). That the Athenians felt themselves to be particularly tardy is less well attested, but see *Ach.*, p. 50. Alan Sommerstein has pointed out to me that 'Athenian' can be used either of women or of ships and that therefore the line may be a reference to the Athenian navy's arrival at various places in 412 BC too late to prevent revolt (cf. Thuc. VIII 17.3; 26-7; 35; 44.3). Mention might also be made of the costly ditherings of Nicias in Sicily.

Paralia: This was the coastal region of Attica.

None of the Salaminians: Salamis is the island that lies just off the coast from Athens, being visible from the city. The Salaminians are said to travel across the narrow straits by skiff. The word used for these small boats is also a term for the sexual position in which the woman is on top, hence Calonice's remarks; 'on the go' and 'they probably will too' (cf. notes pp. 208 and 197).

The Acharnians: Acharnae was a deme to the North-West of Athens and was particularly hard pressed by the invading Peloponnesian army during the war. The women of that deme are expected to be in favour of making peace for the same reasons that its men were for the continuation of hostilities (cf. *Ach.* passim).

Ponchidae: After Salamis and Acharnae the third place mentioned by Lysistrata is Anagyrus, a deme of Attica, which shared its name with a foul smelling plant. Calonice's reply this time makes a play upon the proverbial pungency of the shrub, which grew in the marshes there, but is here translated by the imaginary place name 'Ponchidae'.

p. 183   **Lampito**: This was the name of the wife of Archidamus, the Spartan king, who had led the Peloponnesian invasions into Attica in the early part of the war. The name, however, is probably not used here to recall a specific person. Corinth and Boeotia were both allies of Sparta and bitter enemies of Athens. The stereotype of the Spartan woman is of a strong, sun-tanned female. This was presumably the result of the strict physical training that was expected of women as of men at Sparta.

Sae cuid you: The Spartans spoke in the Doric dialect, which is imitated here by rather imperfect Scots.

If ye were in training...: The Spartan system rigorously trained both males and females to be physically fit. Weaklings were not tolerated, but were exposed at birth. In order to ensure the strongest offspring, women, in accordance with the regulations laid down by Lycurgus, were required to undergo training. 'Rump jumps' probably involved jumping so that one's heels touched one's bottom.

Boeotian...a fertile vale: Once the Spartan has been characterised by her muscular physique, a similar and comic identification is attempted for other nationalities. 'Fertile' describes both the Boeotian land (cf. *Ach.*, p. 89) and the woman's groin. The full humour of this passage is only possible when the different parts of the female anatomy are indicated on the suitably attired male actors. The plucking and shaping of pubic hair was commonly practised by ancient women (cf. p. 185). Not to do so was felt to be careless and slovenly.

She's a braw bonny lass – a Corinthian: Corinth was a wealthy trading state. The stereotypical Corinthian woman is therefore said to be well-endowed.

p. 184   **In Thrace, keeping an eye on our general there**: In the Greek
Eucrates is named; his name being substituted for that of a place.
Nothing is known of him.

Pylos: This fortification on the Peloponnesian coast had long
been in the hands of the Athenians, despite the fact that the Peace of
Nicias (421 BC) had required its return to Sparta. It was recaptured
by the Spartans shortly after 411 BC.

Now the Milesians have rebelled: The people of the Ionian island
of Miletos had revolted from Athenian control in 412 BC encouraged
by Alcibiades and the weakening grip of the Athenian navy after Sicily
(cf. Thuc. VIII 17). According to Diodorus Siculus (VIII 20) Miletos
had a sordid reputation, which is made explicit here by the nature of
its exports.

As leather rations: Dildoes, as also the comic phallus (cf. *Clouds*,
note p. 135), were made of leather (cf. note p. 186).

Even if I had to take off my cloak this day and...: The expected
conclusion to the line is 'fight'. 'Drink' is substituted in accordance
with the drunken and debauched image that women had. (cf. pp. 196-7
and notes pp. 199 and 180). The verb *katatithenai* can mean 'pledge'
or 'pawn' as well as 'take off'. Myrrhine is thus implying that she is
ready to pawn her clothes and give the proceeds to the cause. But
ekpiein is also ambiguous. Far from declaring a resolve 'to
expend/give' all the pawned proceeds to the cause, she hints by the
use of the verb that she intends 'to drink up' all the money, in other
words spend it on drink. The second speaker caps this first pledge by
giving up not just her clothes but half her body.

Like a flatfish: A flat fish, having its eyes on one side, is like a fish
that has been cut in half. This notion is used by the Aristophanes of
Plato's *Symposium* (191D and 205E) to explain his theory of the sexes,
that properly they are two halves of one whole. It is also one that may
have been familiar from sacrifices, which sometimes demanded that
the victim be cut in half. Xerxes, about to set out for Greece, marched
his army through the two halves of a human victim's body (cf.
Herodotus VII 39).

Taygetus: The Spartan swears her allegiance by the heights of
Taygetus, the highest mountain of the range that divides Laconia from
Messenia. The much enjoyed modern pastime of mountaineering was
not one shared by the ancient Greeks. Climbing a mountain
(Bacchants excepted) is an absurd suggestion, even for a Spartan
woman.

We must give up – sex: What Lysistrata in fact instructs them to give up is the penis. In addition to the belief that women were more susceptible to intoxication than men (cf. note on '*Even if I had to take off my cloak this day and...* ') it seems also to have been thought that they were less able to resist sexual temptation. In fact indulgence seems to have been closely associated with women's religious activities.

p. 185 **All we're interested in is having our fun and then getting rid of the baby**: The Greek here makes a more specific reference to the story of Tyro, who bore two sons to Poseidon and tried to conceal her shame by exposing the offspring in a small boat and setting them adrift. The previous line ('The tragic poets are right about us after all') can then be understood as referring to one play in particular, namely *Tyro* of Sophocles.

You're the only real woman among the lot of them: There is a surprise substitution of 'woman' for 'man'.

We're at home, beautifully made up...: Lysistrata's plan here and on pp. 181-2 above would seem to be to drive the men wild with the promise, but not the fulfilment, of sex. In the event the women avoid their husbands. We need not criticise the inconsistency, but perhaps can see in the present speech a tendency to stereotyping and to titillating naughtiness. In the initial scenes the women's complaint was that their husbands were not at home. Now they intend to withhold sexual favours from their husbands who are at home. This inconsistency is similarly unimportant in so far as it needs explanation, but it is a notable example of the combination of inconsistent elements in an Aristophanic play. It arises from the double plot involving both a strike and the occupation of the Acropolis.

Menelaus threw away his sword: Menelaus being about to kill Helen for her infidelity was, so the tradition has it, once again struck by her beauty (cf. Euripides' *Andromache*, ll. 627 ff.). Menelaus, an heroic Spartan king, is an appropriate choice for the Spartan Lampito.

p. 186 **Pherecrates**: This is probably the comic poet and elder contemporary of Aristophanes. The scholia are contradictory, for one says that Pherecrates was the author of this proverb but another finds no evidence for this. The implication, as explained in the scholia, is that the husbands' actions would be in vain since if the strike were effective there would be no other source for their enjoyment. The words of the Greek expression seem to go further, suggesting sexual connotations; 'dog' can be used of the penis and 'to flay' of male sexual arousal. Tough leather (dog skin) was used to make dildoes (cf. note p. 184).

The Athenian riff-raff tae see sense: The Athenian democratic system allowed every citizen the opportunity to vote. The faction at Athens which most strongly supported the continuation of the war was that which represented 'the many' of Athenian politics. Their oligarchic opponents were more favourable to peace on reasonable terms. It is in character to have the Spartan Lampito expressing such a low opinion of the democracy, and not necessarily an indication of Aristophanes' own political feelings. Aside from the fact that these are the words of a Spartan, such criticism of the rabble – that they were unable to make reasonable decisions – is frequent in comedy, as is the vilification of politicians for being debauched.

Not sae lang as their warships have sails: For 'sails' we should more accurately read 'feet' or 'oars' (since the trireme's feet were its banks of oars). Athenian strength rested with its navy. In this also resided the political influence of the people, since the Thetes, the lowest class of Athenian citizens, were oarsmen in the fleet. The political balance could be affected if a large naval expedition caused the Thetes to be absent from home and to be under-represented in the assembly (cf. note p. 192). It is perhaps surprising to find such reverence for the Athenian fleet so shortly after the disastrous Sicilian Campaign. In this respect Aristophanes is being optimistic in the face of great adversity, especially since the Spartans had recently, with Persian help, acquired a fleet to match that of Athens (cf. Thuc. VIII 52-3).

That bottomless fund o' money in Athena's temple: The Acropolis housed the treasury of Athena, whether in the Parthenon or Erechtheum is uncertain. Here Pericles had lodged 1000 talents (Thuc. II 24) which were to be used only under the direst circumstances. Lines 421-2 on p. 197 imply that there was a shortage of oars at this time. In order to stop further shipbuilding the women must occupy the Acropolis.

We're going to occupy the Acropolis: The women intend to occupy the Acropolis because that is where the money is, but it had also been the first target of past revolutionaries (cf. Thuc. I 126 of Cylon's attempted coup). The men of the chorus associate the women's actions with such former events (cf. pp. 190-1).

A SCYTHIAN POLICEWOMAN: She is invented to suit the occasion of a women's meeting. For the Scythian Archers at Athens see *Ach.*, note p. 51.

p. 187 **The one that Aeschylus talks about**: The reference is to *Seven against Thebes* (1. 42) where an oath is sworn by the invaders after the

sacrifice of a bull. The substitution of a sheep here for a bull probably
has sexual connotations.

A full-grown cock: In the Greek text Calonice proposes the
sacrifice of a white horse. The scholiast suggests that a 'white horse'
is a double entendre for penis or that such sacrifices were made by
the Amazons.

Thasian vine's blood: The reputation of this wine for being rich
and dark makes it a good substitute for blood and it is also appropriate
that a ceremony concerning peace should be celebrated with wine and
not blood. Not to add water to wine was felt by the Greeks to be
extravagant and decadent, further adding to the doubtful propriety of
women which has already been noted (cf. note p. 184).

O holy Goddess of Persuasion: The personification of abstract
concepts was common among the Greeks. One of the most powerful
of these was *Peitho* (the goddess of Persuasion), largely because by
her aid much was to be won in all aspects of life; social, political and
personal. In a formal prayer *Peitho* is called upon by the women
because they will need her help in persuading their husbands. Since
she was also believed to be the companion of Aphrodite, her influence
is wisely sought in view of the women's intentions. 'The women will
get their way by arousing and then cheating their husbands. And who
better to appeal to in a matter of arousal than Peitho? With her help,
the women influence first the physical and then the political stance of
men.' (R.G.A. Buxton, *Persuasion in Greek Tragedy: a study of Peitho*,
p. 44). On the 'Loving Cup' see *Ach.*, p. 94 with note.

What lovely red blood!: The wine which has been substituted for
the blood of sacrifice is said, mimicking the terminology of sacrifice,
to flow freely as if propitiously. The zeal with which the women
celebrate the pouring of the fragrant wine and are eager to be the first
to taste it further adds to their wine-loving characterization.

Not unless you draw the first lot: Myrrhine wishes to take the oath
first because this means having the first taste of the wine. But, as was the
practice at a symposium where the master of ceremonies who was
chosen by lot poured the wine and decided upon the drinking order, so
here. There is a conflation of the ideas and practices of drinking and of
taking an oath (cf. *Ach.*, p. 57 with note on 'These three peaces'). We
may note that religious rites, except it would seem the actual sacrifice
of an animal, could thus be imitated on stage without fear of impiety.

p. 188   **The lion-on-a-cheese-grater position**: The actual position is
uncertain. Either this is one with which the ancients would have been
familiar or, as seems more likely, it is a product of Lysistrata's

imagination having been suggested by a lion carved upon the handle of a cheese-grater (cf. Sparkes, *JHS* 1962, p. 132). The latter interpretation is nicely suggestive and it is perhaps to be imagined that, by contrast to the supine position of the woman in the previous line with her legs raised, this is a position in which the woman is like a lioness crouching ready to pounce.

p. 189 **I'll dispose of the sacred remains**: This would be the normal sacrificial procedure, but here it is suggested by Lysistrata for selfish reasons, since she wishes to drink the remaining wine herself. The characterisation of women as craving for alcohol is again emphasized.

No, by Aphrodite...: Her choice of goddess has obvious appropriateness. For the 'impossible' reputation of women see note p. 180 'we're such clever villians'.

The *Parodos* was the sung procession of the chorus along the *eisodos* into the *orchestra*. In this play the chorus is divided in two. Twelve of their number, who are old men, now move slowly from the wings into the *orchestra* carrying bundles of kindling wood and lighted torches. Their progress is not accompanied by the more usual flowing trochaic tetrameters, but by more halting rhythms. They have come to smoke out the women, whose victorious seizure of the Acropolis we have just heard (cf. p. 189). Since the young men are at war, these old men have taken it upon themselves to ward off this threat to the state. They are intensely patriotic and recall their victories in the past (although had they actually taken part in these they would be over one hundred years old). The old women, who formed the second part of the chorus and equalled their male counterparts in number, have prepared themselves with jars of water in order to defend the Acropolis. The entry of the women from the well (cf. p. 193) is accompanied by lively metrical rhythms which contrast the men's approach. They speak more briefly. Although both parties have long been visible to the audience, they do not for a long time see each other (cf. p. 194).

p. 190 **We've kept and fed within our doors**: The traditional picture of women, and one which the old men with their more conservative attitudes here seem to confirm, was that their place was in the home. Our understanding of the role of women in Athenian society is complicated by their representation in tragedy (albeit that of an heroic age) and their participation in religion, where they are not thus confined (cf. J. Gould, 'Law, Custom and Myth: Aspects of the Social Position of Women in Classical Athens', *JHS* 100 1980, pp. 38-59).

Lycon's wife: She is mentioned elsewhere in comedy for her immorality. Her husband Lycon is referred to at *Wasps*, l. 1301.

King Cleomenes: The story is told by Herodotus (V 70-2). A parallel is drawn between the enemies of the democracy in 508 BC and now.

Six whole years: The occupation of the Acropolis by Cleomenes in fact lasted only three days. The ignominious retreat of the Spartans is emphasized by their unkempt appearance at their departure. The fact that he 'hadn't washed for six whole years and had hair all over his face' is also an allusion to the dirtiness of the Spartans whose rough lifestyle was not one that regarded the niceties of personal hygiene highly. The Spartans who appear at the end of the play are similarly roughly bearded (cf. p. 225). Since the Athenians would also have worn beards, the distinction is one of having an untrimmed beard.

p. 191   **We slept before the gates**: The old men identify themselves with the heroic deeds of their ancestors, for even the eldest of the chorus could not have been alive at the time. However, in comedy such impossible longevity is found (cf. p. 208 and *Ach.*, note p. 57 'Real men of Marathon'). This is absurdly comic but also reflects a pride in past achievements. Such an expression of unity with those who fought for the city and its constitution argues for a strong national feeling. It can be detected throughout contemporary Athenian literature. It is here seen to be an obstruction to peace, even after the conflict had turned sour for Athens.

Now the enemies of the gods and of Euripides: 'God detested' was a common comic term of abuse. The chorus of men add 'Euripides detested', since Euripides was a reputed misogynist.

Marathon: For the significance of the battle of Marathon in Athenian history see *Ach.*, note p. 57.

p. 192   **I think a mad dog in disguise has jumped up and bitten my eyes!**: The smoking brazier is representative of the men's wrath as is the stinging it causes in their eyes. For similar metaphors see p. 223 and *Ach.*, p. 63. At *Ach.*, p. 49 the irritation is caused by soap not smoke.

Pallas the Warrior-Maid: Athena was worshipped under many different titles. At the centre of the Acropolis stood the enormous statue of *Athena Promachos* (the warrior). The Parthenon was so called because it was dedicated to *Athena Parthenos* (the maiden). References hereafter to the Maid are to Athena (cf. pp. 193 and 194).

Can the generals in Samos hear us?: The destruction of the fleet that had sailed to Sicily had weakened the naval supremacy of Athens. A consequence of this was the concentration of military and naval strength at Samos to safeguard Athenian control over the allies. With the fleet absent, the political balance was considerably altered (cf. note p. 186), and this resulted in the revolutions that were to follow. Despite their distance from Athens the leaders at Samos still attempted to exert an influence over Athenian affairs.

Our Lady of Victory: To the right of the Propylaea as one approaches this entrance gate of the Acropolis (at which the men are now imagined to be standing), stood the temple of *Athena Nike* (Athena, the goddess of victory). The women had prayed to Persuasion (cf. p. 187); the men pray to Athena Nike. In this way their intentions are made clear.

p. 193   **But at the spring we suffered great delay**: For the purpose of sacrifice water was generally carried to the Acropolis from the Clepsydra, a small spring at the Western end of the Acropolis. As it seems that Aristophanes is here imagining a commonplace for women (that is, the daily morning visit to the spring) a larger secular water source is a more likely meeting place for the women. The major supply of water for public consumption in this area of the city was the Enneacrounus. That this is the site would seem to be confirmed by line 377, p. 195 (cf. note 'A bridal bath').

In the following scene the two semi-choruses come face to face. They would presumably have entered the orchestra separately and have danced apart from each other until this point when they now confront one another. The argument becomes increasingly embittered, a fact reflected in the use of stichomythia and then enjambment. Each side tries to outdo the other in terms of the violence of their threats. At the end the women empty their water jugs over the men and douse their torches.

p. 194   **A Bupalus or two on the jaw**: The men propose to attack the women as the poet Hipponax did Bupalus. This attack was only (as far as we know) verbal, but the words 'on the jaw' make it clear that the men are preparing physical violence. The translation interprets this by punningly using Bupalus as if 'a bop on the jaw'. A fragment of Hipponax does preserve the threat to strike a blow to the eye of Bupalus. The men's target, however, is the mouth, since it is this which the women exercised most.

No dog will ever grab your balls again!: The women knew to hit where it hurt! Perhaps dogs were the ancient equivalent of the zip, their teeth a potent threat. The postman's canine tribulations are a modern comic stereotype.

p. 195   **'There is no beast so shameless as a woman'**: The line may well have occurred in a now lost Euripidean play. Alternatively it may be one which is Euripidean in sentiment (cf. p. 222). The men, unequal to the threats of the women, change the course of the argument.

Put our fire out? You'll see!: It is significant that the single line is divided between two speakers. The same is true of the following lines on this page. This marks the increasing intensity of the argument and indicates, as it were, the face-to-face conflict of the choruses. The long-awaited drenching of the men is being hastened to completion.

A bridal bath: The water for this was traditionally drawn from the Enneacrounus, the 'Nine Springs' (cf. note p. 193). Stratyllis is being sarcastic.

You'll never sit on a jury again: Most modern editors prefer a present tense, ('you are not now sitting on a jury'), the implication being that it is only when sitting on a jury that these old men have any power. From *Wasps* we learn that juries largely consisted of elderly men and that they took great pleasure in their service on these.

Over to you, water!: The women empty the contents of their pitchers over the men. This was probably symbolic, since a pitcher full of water would have been extremely heavy and would have completely drenched the men, making their part in the play hereafter most unpleasant. At a production of *Lysistrata* at Cambridge in 1986 a small amount of water was sufficient to make the action funny and ensure that the women's threats did not end in an anti-climax.

Was it hot?: The water freshly drawn from the spring would have been cold, especially since the Lenaia, at which this play was produced, was held early in the year.

p. 196   **We're watering you to make you grow**: The women's actions have the opposite effect for, as the men's response (accurately translated) shows, they are shrinking and shivering with the cold.

Stop it! Help! Help! Magistrate!: This last line of the men is not found in the Greek text and should be ignored. It is appropriate that the victors in the fight, the women, have the last word.

A magistrate (a *proboulos*, cf. note p. 197) now enters, having heard of the insurrection upon the Acropolis. He is as yet unaware that the women propose a sex strike. His reason for coming to the Acropolis is to collect money from the treasury for the equipping of the fleet (p. 197). If Lysistrata is to be successful in her campaign for peace she must therefore oppose him. When he discovers that the tumult is centred upon an unruly band of women he rashly concludes that they must be involved in some orgiastic religious celebration and uses the occasion to make an attack upon the permissiveness of the modern society which has given such freedom to women. The magistrate attempts to have the women arrested by giving an order to his policemen, but these men are overpowered by the women, leaving the magistrate alone to argue with Lysistrata. In reality (if not in comedy) armed Scythian policemen would not be scared away by unarmed women.

We glimpse in this scene comedy's mockery of the bombastic self-opinionated establishment figure. As the male representative for the continuation of the war he wins no sympathy. Because of his arrogance he is discredited and humiliated, departing the stage a subject of derisive laughter (cf. Lamachus in *Ach*.). His attitude towards women is both disdainful and crude, and even if exaggerated must nonetheless reflect a strand of contemporary thought.

Sabazius and Adonis: Religion was a sphere of public life in which women played a prominent role. They played a major part in the festivals of Athena, the Arrhephonia, the Lenaia, and exclusively celebrated the Thesmophoria and Skira. Besides these, certain foreign cults, like those of Dionysus and – as mentioned here – Sabazius and Adonis, attracted female adherents. This has often been felt to be at odds with the political and social status of women. But it is not difficult to attribute the involvement of women in these religious celebrations to their connection with birth and fertility. (In general see the pioneering work of S.B. Pomeroy, *Goddesses, whores, wives and slaves: women in Antiquity*, pp. 75-8; more recent work in this field has contradicted the myth of matriarchy: cf. M. Lefkowitz, *Women in Greek Myth*, ch. 1.) The worship of Sabazius seems to have been a new introduction to Athens in the 430s; that of Adonis had been known for longer in Greece, his cult coming from Cyprus in the seventh century. Worship of the former involved intoxication, that of the latter was confined to women.

I remember once in the Assembly – Demostratus...: That ill-omens attended the sending of the Sicilian Expedition and that these were linked to the festival of Adonis is confirmed by Plutarch (cf. *Nicias* 13 and *Alcibiades* 18). Worshippers of Adonis bewailed his untimely death upon the rooftops where they also cultivated gardens in his honour (cf. Plato, *Phaedrus* 276B). One might wonder how light-heartedly the Athenian audience would have received this comic portrayal of the woman's intervention at the time of the sending of the expedition in view of the fate that it met. The point made by the *proboulos* is that the failure of husbands to control their wives has disastrous consequences for men. The incident may also be seen to indicate the foolishness of Demostratus and the men who voted the expedition for not having recognized the omens.

p. 197   **Put the pin back in the hole for her**: Two stories are told, emphasizing the way in which Athenian husbands have spoilt their wives and pandered to their worst excesses. The first concerns the mending of a necklace, the second of a shoe strap. References to a goldsmith, a cobbler (both occupations associated like our milkman with adultery), Salamis (cf. note p. 182) and to different sized holes (one that is too large, the other which is too small) make clear the sexual nature of the stories. The husbands' lack of attention to their wives has led to their indulgence in the worst excesses. Again the female stereotype is reinforced.

    The Committee of Ten: Ten *probouloi* were appointed at Athens after the Sicilian disaster to attend to matters of urgency. The immediate need was to rebuild the fleet (Thucydides VIII 1). The Proboulos has come to withdraw money from the treasury upon the Acropolis in order to buy wood for oars. The women have seized the Acropolis with the intention of preventing the use of these funds for the continuation of the war (cf. p. 186).

    By Artemis: Each of the women as they confront the Scythians invoke a goddess: Artemis, who is also heralded as the Bull Goddess, Pandrosus, and Hecate, the giver of light (p. 198). All are virgin deities associated with the Acropolis.

p. 198   **You'll soon be crying out for a cupping-glass!**: Myrrhine means that she will hit them so hard that they will need the use of a cupping-glass to apply the necessary suction to their bruised and swollen bodies.

    Lettuce-seed-pancake-vendors: Aristophanes invents a comically compounded word of thirty one letters with which Lysistrata summons help. The next line has a similarly fanciful word; Innkeepers-bakers-garlic-makers.

p. 199   **Or that women couldn't have any stomach for a fight?**: The magistrate counters by associating the liver with drink, and thus yet again making a jibe at the supposed drunkenness of females (cf. note p. 184 'Even if I had to take off my cloak...').

With the chorus of old men disquieted by the water attack of the old women and the magistrate's Scythian Archers routed by Lysistrata's women, the contest (*agon*) now becomes one of words. It is here that the more serious arguments of the women are set forth, although the banter with the *proboulos* still continues. Lysistrata maintains that the war is the cause of many of the city's problems and that were there internal harmony the state might be strong again. By an analogy with the carding of wool in order to remove its impurities, she suggests a purge in the state. The magistrate continues to deny that women have any part in the man's world. The metaphor of carding wool is given a visual dimension as the *proboulos* is dressed in a woman's clothes and shown how it is done (cf. p. 204).

We want to keep the money safe and stop you waging war: See also p. 186.

p. 200   **Peisander**: He is also mentioned by Aristophanes in *Peace*, l. 394. In *Acharnians* Aristophanes complains about those who seek financial gain from the war (cf. p. 55). It was Peisander who was later to bring the oligarchic demands of those at Samos to Athens.

We've been in charge of all your housekeeping finances for years: The women claim that because they manage the money at home they are equally competent to manage the state's finances (the same claim is made by Praxagora at *Eccl.*, ll. 211-12). What influence the women's claims are likely to have had upon the audience is difficult to assess. Generally commentators feel that the thought of women supervising state treasuries would have been extremely far fetched.

p. 201   **At home**: The woman's place was at home. She took no part in political decision-making but awaited the return of her husband and, with the pleasant smile that was expected of her, would ask of the conclusions reached during the day. The stereotype – the warmed slippers and the 'nice day, darling?' – is not so very different from our own.

Inscribe on the pillar underneath the Peace Treaty: The peace in question is the Peace of Nicias (cf. Thuc. V 47). The inscription written underneath that the Spartans had not abided by the terms was instigated by Alcibiades (Thuc. V 56). See also *Ach.*, p. 82 with note.

I wouldn't have done!: Stratyllis again interrupts. The serious issue is punctuated by the interjections of this blustering old woman. Interjections in *agon* speeches are common. They maintain a lively and humorous atmosphere.

'Let war be the care of menfolk': The quotation is from *Iliad* VI, ll. 490-2 where Homer tells of the confrontation of Hector and Andromache. Much of the passage here is modelled upon that incident in Homer, but there Hector had shown sympathy for his wife's anxiety. The men of Athens, says Lysistrata, have long ignored their wives' feelings.

Listen to us and keep quiet: The women have suggested that they could organize the state as effectively as the men. For once the men should keep silent and listen to the women. What would appear to be a serious comment is now turned into an ocassion for a farcical mockery of the magistrate by the enforced wearing of a woman's attire. Lysistrata will later (pp. 203-4) explain to him how working the wool is analogous to organizing the smooth running of the state. Henderson (Aristophanes' *Lysistrata*, OUP, 1987) notes the similarities between the *proboulos* and Pentheus. (Euripides' *Bacchae* had not yet been produced but the audience will have been familiar with the story from the myth and from earlier dramatizations of it, e.g. by Aeschylus). Both are tyrannical and misjudge an important issue; both are dressed as women and discover that the women who oppose them are not to be trifled with.

p. 202　　**Munching beans**: Women were in the habit (before the days of tobacco, chewing-gum and wine-gums!) of chewing beans while they worked, possibly to relieve the monotony of their weaving or spinning.

That war is the care of the women!: See on p. 201 above. Wool and the spindle are mentioned by Hector as the prerogatives of women (Homer, *Iliad* VI, ll. 490-2).

Come forward, ladies: The chorus of old women now encourage the younger women and especially Lysistrata to press their case, as had the old men the magistrate on p. 199.

p. 203　　**Child of valiant ancestors of stinging nettle stock**: The complex verbal puns of this line are impossible to translate into English. The chorus, in encouraging Lysistrata to be her most stinging, punningly imply her parentage to be that of a jelly fish or nettle.

We will be known as the Peacemakers of Greece: The word used for 'Peacemakers' literally means 'War-disbanders' (*Lysimachai*) and is similar to the pun contained in Lysistrata's name which means 'Army-disbander'. It has been suggested that Lysistrata, whose stately characterisation is closely linked with the Acropolis where she presides and with Athena, is modelled upon an historical figure, namely one Lysimache. As the priestess of Athena, Lysimache would have occupied a seat of honour in the theatre. Lines 991-2 of *Peace* also seem to be a reference to this Lysimache. The references here and in *Peace*, however, are made in passing. There is no need to qualify the characterisation of Lysistrata, which is very carefully drawn within the play, by external considerations (cf. Henderson xxxviii-xl).

No more people clomping round the Market Square in full armour: The war had meant that the residents of the Attic countryside had taken refuge in the city (cf. *Ach.*, p. 52 with note). Since the Sicilian disaster and the occupation of the fortress at Decelea by the Spartans, even more men in armour would have been seen within the city because of the need to garrison the walls continuously (cf. Thuc. VII 28).

A shield with a ferocious Gorgon on it: In *Acharnians* Lamachus is said to carry just such a shield (cf. pp. 74 and 93), but he had died in Sicily in 414 BC. No-one is specifically being referred to here.

That cavalry captain...with his lovely long hair: Long hair was fashionable amongst the upper classes at Athens (*Clouds*, p. 112 and *Knights*, l. 580) and generally at Sparta (Herodotus I 82). The cavalry gentleman is ridiculed for his appearance, his buying of an unappetizing snack from an old street vendor (the shopping was usually done by slaves) and his concealing of this within his helmet.

A Thracian...brandishing his light-infantry equipment: The Thracians provided auxiliary troops to serve in the Athenian army. At *Ach.*, pp. 55-6, it is suggested that they were an unruly rabble.

p. 204   **First...you wash the grease out of it**: The preparation of wool serves as a metaphor for the necessary reconditioning of the state. An excellent guide to this passage will be found in *Aristophanic Poetry* ch. 2 by Carroll Moulton. Lysistrata demonstrates to the *proboulos* the techniques of working wool using the implements he had been given earlier (p. 202). Various groups of people who are troublesome, like the impurities within the untreated wool, are to be removed. It is not easy to be specific about these, but it would seem that the first examples are of social undesirables, the later of political nuisances. The analogy is not without considerable good sense since it wisely sees that the first task is to settle the situation at home before giving consideration to foreign affairs. More commonly such advice is found in the *parabasis* of the play (cf. the metaphor from coinage employed in *Frogs*), but since this comedy has a divided chorus the customary means of directly addressing the audience is missing.

The club members: It would seem that Aristophanes is refering to oligarchic factions within the state who were known to be plotting against the democracy (cf. Thuc. VIII 54). Recent events certainly made this an uncertain time in Athenian politics and subsequent events proved anxieties to be well founded. Thucydides considered that the political divisions at Athens during the war were so counter-productive that they, more than any other reason, led to the defeat of Athens (II 65).

Then you're ready for the carding: The strands of the wool are teased out in preparation for the spinning. The various residents at Athens, both citizens and non-citizens, are to be ready to form a new harmonious state. With the heavy losses which the war had caused there had been discussion about opening citizenship to resident aliens (metics) and others. Even debtors can be admitted provided that they are loyal to the state.

Colonies: The colonists from the mother city became citizens of the colony to which they travelled. Lysistrata calls for an international citizenship which would foster a greater sense of unity. Whether she also meant to include the subject allies in this citizenship is uncertain, but may be presumed if foreigners resident at Athens are to be included as mentioned above.

Can make the People a coat: The cleaned and carefully prepared wool is made into a coat. A new citizen body will thus be constituted which has the best interests of Athens at heart. The donation of the *Peplos* (a cloak) to Athena was the central ceremony of the Panathenaic festival. Thus Lysistrata's proposals, which are essentially based upon the domestic experience of women, are given religious and political significance.

p. 205   **Think of the unmarried ones**: Athenian girls were commonly married while in their teens to men who might often be twice their age (cf. Pomeroy, p. 64). But the urgency of the women's plea is not simply that the young are growing old, but that they are unmarried – an unthinkable status for a woman at Athens.

It's high time that you died: The insinuation is that, far from being capable of sexual intercourse, the magistrate is so senile that he could be considered a corpse. At the end of the first section of the *agon* the magistrate was dressed as a woman, here he is treated as a corpse and prepared for burial. We are again reminded of the discomfiture of Pentheus (cf. note p. 201 'Listen to us and keep quiet').

The fillets all red – and here is the wreath for your head: Both of these are funerary decorations. But Henderson points out that two garlands are given to the *proboulos*: one, an appropriate funerary offering; the other, a garland he has been wearing since being dressed as a woman. To add insult to injury, he is being treated as a dead woman.

We'll be with you early the day after tomorrow: Traditionally the third day marked further rituals and offerings associated with the burial of the dead person.

The magistrate now leaves to report his humiliation to the other *probouloi*, while Lysistrata and her young companions depart for the Acropolis. The two choruses remain, once again confronting each other as they had before the beginning of this scene. The men sing, after which their leader makes an address. There follows the women's song and their leader's response. The pattern is then repeated. The men see themelves as stalwart defenders of the *demos* and declare their resolve to ward off these 'Amazonian' women. The women defend their cause by reminding the men of their major role in the religious life of the city and of their providing male offspring. The men, they claim, have squandered the city's resources and been responsible for the most foolish decisions.

p. 206   **Take off your coats**: Such a call to fellow chorus members was common preparatory to a dance (cf. *Ach.*, p. 77).

It stinks of Tyranny!: It was Harmodius and Aristogeiton who at the end of the 6th century had struck the blows for freedom when they assassinated Hipparchus, the brother of the tyrant Hippias (cf. note on 'I'll bear my sword within a myrtle bough' below). Since then Athens had not only been proud of her democracy but also a bit paranoid about it (cf. *Wasps*). Those who opposed the democracy, who had oligarchic sympathies or who were prepared to negotiate with Sparta, could find themselves charged with engendering tyranny. It would appear that such charges, at least in comedy, were often associated with the demagogues, like Cleon, who felt it their duty to guard the state against subversive elements.

To seize our jury fees: Jury service at Athens was paid. Although the amount was meagre (2 obols was the rate set by Pericles, which was raised to 3 obols probably by Cleon), in theory it allowed everyone to be involved. Since the law courts were often used to try political cases, their democratic significance was great. The seizure of the juryman's pay is thus a threat to the democracy. In practice (at least judging from what we learn from Aristophanes), it was old men (like the men of the chorus) who, being supported by their sons, were glad to earn this sum of money for themselves.

Sparta's wolves: The wolf was proverbially not to be trusted, as were Sparta's motives.

'I'll bear my sword within a myrtle bough': This is the first line of an ancient drinking song which celebrated the exploits of Harmodius and Aristogeiton (cf. note on 'It stinks of Tyranny' above). Their killing of Hipparchus, the brother of the tyrant Hippias, in 514 BC was remembered as a significant moment in the establishment of a democracy at Athens. Their statues stood at the highest part of the

Agora, indicating the respect they were granted. According to Thucydides (VI 53-9) the two were lovers and the killing of Hipparchus arose from a personal grudge. For the importance of the emphasis given to the tyrannicides see note p. 228.

p. 207 **I became a girl priestess in the Erechthean temple of the Maid**: Young girls of aristocratic birth were chosen to serve Athena (here referred to as the Maid, cf. note p. 192) for the duration of a year. Those chosen were responsible for the weaving of the new *peplos* for the cult statue of Athena housed in the temple of Athena Polias (the Erechtheum later served this purpose but at this time was still under construction). They were not priestesses but assistants.

I made flour in the mill: The flour was used to make sacrificial cakes. Again, young girls from the leading families would have been granted this honour of serving the goddess. In reply to the men, the women boast their high social status and claim that their religious devotion reflects their fundamental support for the state.

To Brauron town…the procession as the Bear: Brauron, situated on the South East coast of Attica, was famed for its temple of Artemis, at which the celebrations involved young girls dressed as bears. The yellow gown was often worn on ceremonial occasions (cf. note p. 181). Vase paintings recovered from the precinct of the goddess at Brauron depict girls both in skins and naked. Some form of initiation was presumably being practised (cf. E. Simon, *Festivals of Attica*, pp. 83-8).

She…hits the men's leader: This reciprocates the blow (actual or threatened) of Stratyllis on p. 206.

p. 208 **Let's show we're men not sandwiches**: The Greek word used to express their being wrapped in clothes also describes the sandwiching of delicacies in a fig leaf pancake.

Party-sandalled men: 'White (*leuko*) footed' is an emendation for the unmetrical 'wolf (*luko*) footed'. Both readings are obscure but there may be a pun intended even after the emendation has been made on metrical grounds. Once again the old men return to the expulsion of the tyrant. The opposition was led by Cleisthenes of the Alcmaeonid family ('The tyrants' foes in days of yore'), whose family motif may well have been the wolf or wolf's foot. Alternatively 'whitefeet' may refer to people who do not get their (hands) feet dirty – aristocrats perhaps, like the Alcmaeonids. Ironically the old men call upon aristocrats to help them defend the democracy.

Those days when we were men: Like the old men of the chorus of *Achamians* these old men keep harping back to past victories. This no doubt reflects the pride which was attached to the triumphs won at the turn of the century, but may also characterize the nostalgia of the elderly.

Fight against the city's fleet: *Plein* 'sail' and *naumachein* 'fight a sea battle' are both used of being on top during sexual intercourse (cf. note p. 182 'None of the Salaminians'). Riding, an image employed in the next line, is one we share, although in Greek it does not imply that the male is on top.

That Carian queen: The story of the Carian queen, Artemisia, who helped Xerxes when he invaded in 480 BC is told by Herodotus VII 99 and VIII 87-8.

The Amazonian cavalry engaging Athens' king: The expulsion of the Amazons, the legendary female warriors, by Theseus (the king of Athens) was a popular subject of art and literature. The mythical event was often used to prefigure the Persian invasion of Attica.

The Holy Twain: The reference is to Demeter and Persephone. The women's reply balances the words of the men (men p. 208; women
p. 209 p. 209).

Pointing to a well known politician in the audience: The subject of Stratyllis' scorn is more likely to be the old men and, in particular (since the singular (you) is used), the chorus leader. The verb used to express 'pass a motion' is one that refers to a collective decision of the assembly. We do not then need to suppose a reference to a member of the audience.

The folks next door: From what follows the Boeotians are implied.

Hecate: As a goddess who protected the home she was especially worshipped by women.

A rich Boeotian eel: A delicacy like the Copaic eel imported from Boeotia was in exceedingly short supply because of the war (cf. p. 181 and *Ach.*, p. 89). The comic surprise of this line is that the eel is personified.

You Know Who's decrees: She means the decrees of the Athenian people, but by implication the questionable influence of the demagogues over the assembly is hinted at.

Greek theatre rarely calls attention to the passage of time, but here, five days after the earlier scenes, we see the effects of the women's strike. The audience has been kept in suspense about the effects while the dispute over the occupation of the Acropolis has been staged. The revelation (p. 210) parodies the language of tragedy and further delays the news. The women are finding it difficult to abstain from sexual intercourse as they had promised. Since some of the women have attempted to break out of the Acropolis, Lysistrata has to encourage her followers. Women's stereotypical weaknesses are again emphasized.

p. 210   *In tragic tones*: The use of stichomythia (line by line division of speakers) is a parody of tragic practice, where a crisis from within is often revealed by a rapid cross-questioning of this sort. It is possible and is suggested in the scholium that these lines actually parody a scene from a Euripidean play.

Sex-starvation: Aristophanes comically uses a word which suggests that the women have an illness and thus creates the necessary bathos for the revelation of the truth and the ending of the tragic language.

Clearing out the stopped-up hole in the wall near Pan's Grotto: The women are trying to escape the Acropolis and relieve their sexual frustrations. There were numerous caves on the side of the Acropolis, but the double entendre of the Greek words for 'clearing out' and 'hole' make evident the sexual innuendo. A second deserter tries to escape by using a rope and a third by flying down on the back of a sparrow. The sparrow was commonly associated with Aphrodite and its name used in slang for the phallus.

p. 211   **Aiming straight for the nearest pimp shop**: The Greek has 'to the house of Orsilochus' whom the scholia identify as a brothel owner.

I've got some fleeces there from Miletus: Milesian wool was of high quality and therefore very expensive.

I'll only spread it out on the bed: The woman omits the word for 'it' and hence the line can be interpreted in two ways. This is also true of the second woman's speech – 'as soon as I have stripped it off'.

My flax, my Amorgian flax!: Again, an expensive commodity is the reason for the woman's desire to leave. The flax is possibly the product of the island of Amorgos, but it may be so named because of the expensive dye with which it is coloured.

Without taking the bark off: The phraseology may be sexual. Masturbation is hinted at in similar terms on p. 186 (cf. note on 'Pherecrates') and in the lines below.

p. 212   **There is an oracle**: During the Peloponnesian war oracles and other prophetic signs were prevalent (Thuc. II 8) and often used by politicians to support their policies. Aristophanes was critical of this (*Peace*, ll. 1043 ff., *Birds*, ll. 959 ff., *Wasps*, ll. 799-800). Oracles also play an important part in tragic drama where they introduce a divine dimension into the action of the play. Their treatment in tragedy is more reverent, but interestingly Sophocles' *Philoctetes* shows a similar manipulation of the terms of an oracle in time of war as best suits the interests of one side. Modern politicians do much the same when quoting the forecasts of statisticians or political think-tanks; perhaps, one might add, with little more credibility than their predecessors. Oracles were commonly transmitted in poetic form.

When the swallows escape from the hoopoes: The hoopoe's pursuit of the swallow is an allusion to the myth of Tereus who continued to chase Procne even after both had been metamorphosed. In the new order of things the oracle declares that the roles will be reversed. The birds' names may here be being used as terms for the male and female genitals.

The semi-choruses take turns to restate their cases, this time using mythological examples. The men recall the story of Melanion, who had despised women's company. The women retort with an account of Timon, who detested men. Both myths are in fact considerably adapted to suit the arguments of each side: the old men ignore Melanion's successful wooing of the 'hard to get' Atalanta, the women do not mention Timon's detestation of women no less than men. This choral interlude is a preparation for the continuing battle of the sexes which follows and postpones a little longer the revelation of the effects of the strike upon the men.

p. 213   **A wise young man**: His name, Melanion, is given in the Greek.

p. 214   **Myronides** and **Phormio**: The former was a successful Athenian general by land (cf. Thuc. I 105 and 108), the latter by sea (cf. Thuc. II 80 f.).

    His mother...a sister of the Furies: The Furies or Erinyes were terrifying avenging deities. Their characterization in an Aeschylean play was said to have frightened women into miscarriages.

    Oh, how I shriek!: The men's response is sarcastic.

    With utmost care and frequently our triangles are singed: It was considered slovenly for a woman to allow her pubic hair to be untrimmed (cf. pp. 183 and 185). The women's statement here contrasts that of the men earlier (cf. the men's speech on p. 214).

From the walls of the Acropolis, represented by the roof of the *skene* building, Lysistrata sees a young man hurrying towards the Propylaea. He is clearly suffering from the effects of the sex strike. He is Cinesias, the husband of Myrrhine, with whom he is desperately eager to meet. Lysistrata increases his expectations and enflames his passions by her talk about his wife. When she appears on the battlements Cinesias pleads that she come down to him. He has brought their baby to make his appeal even more effective. At first she refuses, but eventually she comes down. When husband and wife meet, he tries to persuade her to come home with him, but she refuses because she is under oath. She allows the lustful Cinesias to believe that she is willing to gratify his desires but increases his urgency by her excuses and delays until he promises that he will think about voting for peace. She then promptly leaves him.

p. 215   **The Mysteries of Aphrodite:** A euphemism for sexual intercourse.

The shrine of Chloe: This small shrine was to the South-West of the Acropolis.

Keep him on toast: The Greek verb *optan* 'toast' could be used of arousing sexual passion.

I certainly am!: At this point Cinesias gestures in the direction of his hugely enlarged phallus.

p. 216   **Cinesias from Paeonidae:** Paeonidae was the name of a small Attic deme but is also suggestive of the verb *paiein* 'dash' or 'strike' which could be used of having sexual intercourse. Cinesias' name sounds like *kinein* which also has an obscene translation. Henderson says that Cinesias effectively announces himself as 'Mr Screw from Bangtown'.

She can't eat an egg or an apple: It was traditional to toast absent friends in this way.

'The rest are nothing to my Cinesias!': Again there is a pun upon the husband's name, cf. note on 'Cinesias from Paeonidae' above.

I'm permanently rigid: Cinesias laments the absence of his wife in a tragic manner. His final words are deliberately crude.

I love him, I love him!: Myrrhine's words are meant to be a cry to the other women, but of course they are also intended to heighten Cinesias' excitement.

p. 217   **The rites of Aphrodite:** cf. note p. 215.

Pan's grotto: See notes pp. 180 and 210. It was here that Apollo raped Creusa (cf. Euripides *Ion*, ll. 10-13).

p. 218   **How am I supposed to purify myself before going back into the Acropolis?:** Purity was important when visiting a sanctuary. Sexual intercourse and childbirth (cf. p. 211) were reasons for exclusion. Those who were ritually unclean would have to purify themselves before entering. The waters of the Clepsydra on the approach to the Acropolis were used for this purpose (cf. note p. 193).

By Apollo: Apollo was usually invoked by men. It is appropriate that his is the name on Myrrhine's lips because of his connection with Pan's grotto (cf. note p. 217).

She goes into the Acropolis: Henderson, rightly I think, suggests that on each occasion Myrrhine goes to Pan's grotto represented by an exit to the left or right to fetch the various articles needed. Her last exit will be to the Acropolis (p. 220) through the centre doors of the *skene*. Her departure via a different route will then be clearly understood by the audience to be final. Alternatively we may suppose that Myrrhine on each occasion collects the articles from within the central doors of the *skene* and that her final exit is indicated by the closing of the doors behind her.

p. 219   **This is a Heracles' supper**: See *Wasps*, l. 60 and Euripides' *Alcestis*, ll. 747 ff. The gluttonous Heracles was often shown waiting for and sometimes not receiving a meal.

This positively reeks of prevarication: In *Acharnians* Dikaiopolis, judging the value of the peaces that had been brought to him, uses a similar metaphor (cf. *Ach.*, p. 57).

Take this bottle...I've got one already and it's fit to burst: The bridesmaid in *Acharnians* who comes to Dikaiopolis wishing to collect some peace carries just such a small bottle (*alabastos*). With the liquid contained in the vessel the bride is to anoint the bridegroom's penis (pp. 97-8). *Alabastoi* were used by women to keep perfumes. Perhaps because of their size and shape, or perhaps because of a common use for their contents, they were associated with the phallus and may have been used as dildoes.

p. 220   **I'll...She's gone**: Cinesias does not promise to vote for peace, he in fact says 'I will deliberate (about it)'. It is no wonder then that Myrrhine runs off.

Cinesias proclaims his anguish in the manner of a tragic hero. The two semi-choruses interrupt with their comments. The comedy is enhanced by the bathos with which the parody of tragedy is undercut.

p. 220   **It's clear, my poor lad, that you're in a baddish way**: Although it is not apparent in translation, the chorus mimic a tragic chorus' expression of pity, but the pathos of the sentiments is greatly and comically exaggerated.

What heart, what soul, what bollocks could long endure this plight?: The formulation is tragic but the introduction of 'bollocks' is bathetic.

She's a heroine...A heroine you call her?: It is preferable to attribute the word of praise to Cinesias and the surprised question that follows to the men of the chorus. An isolated interfection from the women's chorus is out of place. A significant point in the play has now been reached: Cinesias is the first husband to succumb to the desire for his wife, but the others will soon follow and peace will be made. His passion for his wife is evident in the prayer which follows (cf. p. 221).

I'll tell you just what I would really like to see: Most modern commentators rightly ascribe these lines to Cinesias. The old men are past having erections. Furthermore, since Cinesias is probably to remain on stage to meet the Spartan herald (cf. note on ll. 980-1013, pp. 221-2) this passage ensures there is no break in the action.

p. 221   **Where suddenly she finds that there still is more in store**: A curse is invoked upon Myrrhine because of the anguish she has caused. This again parodies tragedy, but instead of her being dashed to the ground as one would have expected, the formula is broken by the prayer that she may receive an immodestly different fate, but one welcome to the male concerned!

A Spartan herald obviously suffering from the effects of the strike, but desperately trying to conceal it, now enters. There is an opportunity for yet more jokes about the men's predicament before the process of reconciliation is begun. Some discrepancy exists over the identity of the speaker with whom the herald converses. The scholiast suggests that this is the *proboulos* whom we met earlier, but it seems more likely that it is Cinesias since he had been left erect by Myrrhine. It is appropriate that he should meet with a Spartan counterpart also likewise suffering and that he should be instrumental in the making of peace following his promise to his wife.

p. 221   **Where are the lairds o' the Athenian council?**: The Spartan herald speaks in the Doric dialect (cf. note p. 183 'Sae cuid you'). Being unsure of the Athenian constitution he initially asks for the *gerousia* (the council at Sparta). This council was composed of 30 men whose number included the two Spartan kings. The Athenian *prytaneis* (cf. *Ach.*, note p. 50) for which the herald asks in the second instance numbered 50. Although constitutionally similar they were very differently chosen. The members of the *gerousia* came from influential Spartan families and were (the two kings excluded) over 60 years of age.

It's a standard Spartan cipher rod: For a description of how this supposed means of secret communication between Spartan generals worked see Plutarch *Lysander* 19. Doubt has recently been cast upon this in a recent paper by T. Kelly (cf. Eadie and Ober (eds) *The Craft of the Ancient Historian*, Lanham MD, 1985). Most probably the *skutala* here is just a walking stick (cf. Sommerstein, *Birds*, l. 1283). The herald tries to conceal his erection, but his Athenian counterpart ('Yes, and so is this') is not deceived.

p. 222   **Things ha' reached a total cock-up**: A similar double entendre is found in the Greek.

    We canna get hold o' Pellene: That Pellene was a whore is an inference from the present passage, based upon a supposition of the scholiast. Otherwise the reference may be to Pellene, an Achaean ally of Sparta (Thuc. II 9), whom the Spartans had tried to persuade to send ships against the Athenians (Thuc. VIII 3). Henderson suggests that since the context requires a sexual meaning, Pellene is a Laconian word for the vagina.

The departures of the Spartan herald to fetch ambassadors and of the Athenian to advise the council mark the beginning of the reconciliation. This is continued in the following exchanges of the semi-choruses. The women offer to help the old men put on their cloaks which they had taken off earlier (cf. pp. 206-7). They extract bugs (a symbol of anger) from their eyes and give them kisses. Once united, the chorus sings of the benefits of goodwill and generosity. The invitations to share wealth and food are deliberately lavish and follow a pattern commonly found in comedy (cf. *Eccl.*, ll. 1144 ff.; *Peace,* ll. 1115 ff., Plautus *Rudens*, ll. 1418 ff.), where an extravagant promise is unfulfilled.

p. 223   **I'll take that gnat out of your eye**: The stinging of the gnat is a metaphor for the anger of the old men, just as is the stinging of the smoke on p. 191.

    It must be from the Marsh of Marathon: Marathon, the site of the famous victory of the Greeks over the Persians in 490 BC, was on the North-East coast of Attica. Much of the area is marshy and is the habitat of mosquitoes.

    We can't live with you, we can't live without you: The concept was proverbial and at least as old as Hesiod (cf. *Works and Days*, l. 58 and *Theogony*, ll. 600 ff.).

p. 224   **We rather think you've had enough of toil and tribulation**: This refers both to the conflict which has been enacted and to the hardships of the last years of the Peloponnesian War. The chorus invite the audience to forget their troubles for a moment. The jest which follows need not refer to the state paucity of resources but simply coincides with a conventional pattern of humour (cf. introductory note to this section).

If anyone is short of drachs: 'If anyone wants a little money' is followed by the ridiculously generous offer of 200 or more drachmas, a sum which would modestly keep a family for the best part of a year.

You will never need to pay it back again: This helps to explain why the offer was so generous. There will be no need to repay the loan, since there is no money to be lent. The Greek has it that the loan need not be repaid 'if ever a day of peace should dawn'. This would seem to suggest that in reality (despite the arguments of the play) no such day was near.

I'm entertaining some friends from Carystus tonight: Carystus, a city in the South of Euboea, had long been an ally of Athens. It would seem from p. 229 that the Carystians had earned a reputation for their ill manners and perhaps also for their sexual activity. There may be significance in the fact that the city's name resembles a word used for the testicles.

p. 225   **There's just one thing**: Anticipation of a splendid feast is heightened by the sumptuous description of the food and preparations. As with the loan, expectations are dashed in the final line.

The Spartan ambassadors arrive to make peace. They are soon followed by negotiators from Athens. Noticeably it is the Spartans who first ask for peace. The remarkable speed of their journey (they were only summoned on p. 222) is like that of Amphitheus in *Acharnians* (cf. pp. 54 and 57).

p. 225   **Our bearded Spartan friends**: Spartans grew their hair and wore their beards long (cf. note p. 190 'six whole years' and *Wasps*, ll. 476-7).

Carrying a pig-pen under there: The choice of a pig-pen may be deliberate in view of the unkempt stereotype of the Spartans (cf. p. 190).

Definitely a case of dropsy: The Athenian officials, because of the way they are bent over and clutching their clothes away from their erections in order that they might not be noticed, in the Greek are likened to wrestlers crouching as they fight. Because of their posture they are said to have an athlete's afflictions, (*asketikon*: 'pertaining to an athlete') with a pun upon the word *askiten* 'dropsy'.

We shall all end up screwing Cleisthenes: He was a favourite butt for Aristophanic jokes because of his effeminacy (cf. p. 206 and *Clouds*, p. 127). At *Ach.*, p. 54, he is also made fun of in an athletic context.

I shouldn't do that if I were you: The Spartan ambassadors are advised not to remove their cloaks lest they suffer the same mutilation as the 'Hermae', for which see Sommerstein's note. An account of the damage done to the 'Hermae' is given by Thucydides (VI 27-9), who, however, does not mention the genitals.

p. 226   **By the Twa Gudes**: They are Castor and Pollux (cf. p. 234).

Lysistratus: It matters not who is summoned provided that he or she has the power to end the strike. There is a pun upon Lysistrata's name, for the end of the strike will be occasioned by the ending of the war and the disbanding of the armies (cf. note p. 203).

Lysistrata enters to supervise negotiations for peace. She brings with her Reconciliation (cf. *Ach.*, p. 94), personified as a very attractive naked woman and embodying in her physical and sensory beauty the benefits of peace. The Athenians and the Spartans can scarcely wait to sample her delights. Thus the sex strike is brought to an end, with the Spartans in their desperation conceding more than they would have been prepared to do in reality. The negotiations with their sexual nature are far from reality, and this type of frivolous ending is common enough in Aristophanes. The reconciliatory and celebratory nature of the final scenes, which recall the festive context of the play (cf. the drunken festivities of *Ach.*, especially note p. 104, where the dramatic and festive contexts coincide), once again presents the central issues but in such a way as to win dramatic approval. The characterization of Reconciliation, while reminding the audience of the desirability of peace, avoids contentious issues. Since all actors are male, female nudity was represented by actors wearing tights with breasts and pubic hair added. Nudity was commonly shown (cf. *Wasps*, ll. 1342 ff., *Thesm.*, l. 1174).

Mighty lady with a mission: Since the English which Sommerstein provides here is not a translation (cf. his note), it is as well to provide one:

> 'Hail, bravest woman of all. Now, now is the time you must show your diverse qualities; your forcefulness and compassion, your down-to-earth nobility, your severity and your kindness. For the Greek leaders have been won over by your charm and are now met together....'

p. 227   **Try that leather thing**: The phallus, like the dildoe, was made of leather (cf. p. 184 and *Clouds*, note p. 135).

I am a woman, but I am not brainless: The common assumption was that women were ignorant (cf. *Frogs*, l. 949, Euripides' *Andromeda*, ll. 364-5). A woman with intelligence is therefore to be feared (cf. Euripides' *Medea*).

Thermopylae: The Amphictyonic League celebrated festivities at Thermopylae known as the Pulaia. Lysistrata names two other major Panhellenic centres (Olympia and Delphi) at which festivities and competitions were held. A truce allowed safe conduct to all who attended these occasions.

Although the Mede is at our gates: Lysistrata tries to encourage Panhellenic unity by suggesting that their enemy is Persia and that the Athenians and Spartans should be visited in opposition to her. The Persians were indeed 'knocking at the gate' since the Persian satraps of Asia Minor were becoming increasingly involved in the fighting out of the war in the Aegean. There may therefore be an indirect reproach of the Peloponnesians for their negotiations with Persia (cf. Thuc. VIII 5.4).

How Pericleidas came to Athens: Historical detail is here carefully edited just as was myth earlier (cf. p. 213). In 464 BC a disastrous earthquake devastated Sparta and led to a revolt of the helots. The hard-pressed Spartans sought the aid of their allies, who then included the Athenians according to the alliance that had been made against the Persians in 481 BC. Pericleidas was sent to Athens. His pleas for assistance were well received by Cimon but opposed by Ephialtes and the radical democrats. The advice of Cimon prevailed and he left for Sparta with a considerable contingent of hoplites (cf. Thuc. I 102) which numbered, according to Aristophanes, four thousand (cf. p. 228). The siege of Mount Ithome, where the helots had taken a stand, proved to be more difficult than expected and the Spartans, fearing the Athenian presence and their connivance with the helots, dismissed them. The ignominious return of Cimon (he had not saved Sparta as Lysistrata suggests) led to his ostracism in 462/1 BC. This incident was significant in the worsening of the relationship between Athens and Sparta (cf. Thuc. I 102.2, 'This expedition was the occasion for the first open quarrel between Athens and Sparta'), but it is recalled by Lysistrata to remind the Spartans of the support they had formerly received from Athens.

In scarlet uniform: Scarlet was the colour of Spartan uniforms (cf. *Ach.*, note p. 63 and Herodotus I 152). It humorously contrasts with Pericleidas' pallid complexion.

p. 228 **Poseidon with his earthquake**: For the association of Poseidon with earthquakes and the reason for the supposed divine displeasure which occasioned this disaster see *Ach.*, note p. 71.

Cimon: Aristophanes' political sympathies may lie with the conservative democrats, for it is they who seem to receive the most favourable comment in his comedies (cf. G.E.M. de St Croix, *The Origins of the Peloponnesian War*, pp. 361-2 and 367).

Is it then just to ravage Athens' land?: In the early years of the war King Archidamus had annually led his Spartan troops into Attica, destroying the crops. In 413 BC King Agis had permanently garrisoned a stronghold within Attica at Decelea from where he plundered the countryside.

She's a fine bottom: Comically, the Spartan's thoughts are elsewhere. He is admiring Reconciliation (cf. the dialogue which follows).

Until the Spartans came in force: Lysistrata has lectured the Spartans upon their need to see the Athenians as their friends and has cited the Athenian assistance given at Ithome, conveniently omitting the details which do not suit her argument. She now turns to the Athenians, reminding them of the help which the Spartan Cleomenes gave in driving the tyrant Hippias from Athens in 510 BC. Thucydides confirms the role of the Spartans in the expulsion of the tyrant (cf. VI 53 ff. 'The Athenians knew it was not they and Harmodius that had put an end to the tyranny, but the Spartans'). Elsewhere emphasis is laid upon the part played by Harmodius and Aristogeiton in assassinating Hipparchus in 514 BC (cf. note p. 206) and of the Alcmaeonid family in using the Delphic oracle to win Spartan support in 510 BC (cf. Herodotus I 59-64; V 55-65 and 94-5; Aristotle *Constitution of Athens* 19). Lysistrata's account of the events suits her purpose here. She conveniently forgets to tell of Cleomenes' actions against Cleisthenes in 508 BC and of his ignominious withdrawal from Athens on that occasion (cf. note p. 190).

Nor I a shapelier cunt: The asides (cf. also 'She's a fine bottom' above) comically interrupt Lysistrata's words, showing that neither side has been paying attention but that they are engrossed in lusting over the beautiful body of Reconciliation. The Spartans, who had a reputation at Athens for preferring anal intercourse, gloat over her 'bottom' as the translation coyly puts it, the Athenians choose the vagina.

Pylos: The capture in 425 BC of Pylos, a promontory on the Western coast of the Peloponnese, was a major success for the

Athenians (cf. Thuc. IV 2-41). The Spartans lost many men in the attempt to recover it and suffered the desertion of many helots here. By pointing to the girl's bottom the Spartan ambassador will have made clear the double entendre.

p. 229 **Who will we have left to stimulate?**: There is a play upon the double meaning of *kinein* 'stir up'/'arouse sexually'/'have intercourse'.

All the Echinian Triangle: Echinus on the North West coast of the Malian gulf upon which Thermopylae stands was controlled by the Spartans. Its strategic importance was probably insignificant, but the name is cited because it is suggestive of the word for a wide-mouthed jar. In this context attention is being drawn to the pubic region of Reconciliation, hence the translation 'Triangle'. When this negotiator claims 'The Malian gulf...the one round behind', one might assume that this refers to the anus, but since this has already been reserved by the Spartan (cf. p. 228), we must suppose that the vulva is the gulf to which reference is being made.

The Long Walls of Megara: These walls had been built by the Athenians in 459 BC between Megara and its seaport, Nisea (cf. Thuc. I 103). They were partly dismantled by the Megarians in 423 BC (cf. Thuc. IV 109), but Nisea remained under Athenian control. Such long walls connecting an inland city to its seaport (as Athens to Piraeus) were termed the 'legs' of the city.

I'm ready to go back to my husbandry now: Reconciliation occasions a return to the tending of the land which had been abandoned because of the war. It will also mean a return to wives. Agricultural terminology aptly translates both instances, since it is often a metaphor for sexual intercourse (cf. *Ach.*, note p. 95).

This song of the chorus continues the theme of lines 1043-71. Generous promises are made and are comically found to be worthless. In the first instance a box supposedly containing embroideries, garments and gems is shown at the last moment to be empty. In the second a sack full of provisions is guarded by a ferocious dog (cf. introductory note on ll. 1014-71, pp. 222-5).

While a banquet is being held, and before all the banqueters emerge, Aristophanes provides a brief parody of a commonly staged scene. However, doubt remains over its enactment. Sommerstein (following Rogers) introduces two layabouts who demand to be allowed to join the party. Others imagine that those at the gates are passive homosexuals (they wear their hair long – a sign of effeminacy) who have come expecting a good time with the Spartans (cf. notes on p. 228), or that they are slaves. Henderson, rightly I think, suggests that the scene is a reversal of the usual gate-crasher routine and that the lines in question are spoken by annoyed negotiators trying to get out of the party. The doorkeeper is then unnecessary for the scene and the speakers are two revellers leaving the party. The success of the festivities is on everyone's lips.

p. 231   **That's an absolute comic cliché**: It is the same today. As the custard pie is about to be thrown, the audience is asked for their approval.

We couldn't be as stupid as we are when we're sober: *Acharnians* emphasizes thematically how war and wine are antithetical.

'Telamon' and 'Cleitagora': These were the titles of drinking songs sung in turn by guests after dinner. It was customary to follow the previous singer with a piece that appropriately advanced the theme of the last. Not to do so would be an indication of poor taste as well as of bad manners. Were we to live enjoying our wine, says the speaker, such small matters of etiquette would not offend. The same attitude should be applied to issues great and small.

Tak the pipes, and I'll dance a reel: The Greeks had a form of bagpipes (cf. Herodotus IV 2 and *Ach.*, p. 88), but since they were associated with nations other than the Athenians the playing of these in the *exodos* of a comedy would have been a novelty. The reel (*dipodia*, a Spartan dance) which the Spartan ambassador proposes would probably also have been a first for the Athenian stage.

The Spartan ambassador sings and dances. He recalls the glorious past of the Athenians and the Spartans, remembering the victory of the former at Artemisium and the stalwart defence of Thermopylae by the latter. That the two great powers of Greece should stand together was the argument of Lysistrata on pp. 227-8.

p. 232   **Holy Memory**: An invocation to the Muses was customary at the commencement of a song. *Mnemosyne* (Memory) was the mother of the Muses (cf. Hesiod, *Theogony*, ll. 53-4 and 915 ff.).

Artemis the Virgin Queen: Artemis (*Agrotera* – the huntress is the title she is given in the Greek) is chosen because of her association in both the Spartan and the Athenian minds with war.

The chorus invite the blessings of the gods. Firstly the Graces, associated with dancing and charm; then Apollo the healer, followed by Artemis his sister, Hera and then Bacchus/Dionysus, in whose honour the dramatic competitions were staged. Next Zeus and finally Aphrodite, whose influence over events has been the greatest (cf. pp. 187, 203 and 215).

p. 233   **Well, gentlemen**: This speech is now commonly attributed to an Athenian ambassador because, among other reasons, Lysistrata implies on p. 229 that her mission is completed. Nevertheless, it does seem appropriate that Lysistrata should preside over the reunion of couples in view of her past endeavours to separate them (cf. Sommerstein, *CR* 1986, pp. 203-4).

O let it be that we may win the victory: The cries of the chorus celebrate the victory of Lysistrata but also anticipate the victory of the play (cf. *Ach.*, p. 104).

The chorus dance joyfully out: It would be unprecedented for a chorus to leave the stage before the end of the play.

The preceding celebration of victory might usually have been expected to conclude the play, but Aristophanes chooses to finish with another Spartan song (cf. p. 232). The content and style of this second piece are more emphatically Spartan.

p. 234   **Phoebus**: In the Greek Apollo is referred to by his cult centre at Amyclae in Laconia.

In her temple brazen let Pallas hear: Athena was worshipped on the Athenian Acropolis and also on the Acropolis at Sparta (cf. *Pausanias* III 17.1-3).

Castor and Polydeuces: They were the twin sons of Zeus and Leda (cf. *Homeric Hymn* 33.1), their mortal father being Tyndareus. They were closely associated with rites of initiation for young boys at Sparta.

Leda's beauteous daughter...Helen: She was the sister of Castor and Polydeuces. In myth she was the beautiful bride of Menelaus, the king of Sparta, who was abducted by Paris (*Iliad* III 87). But she was also the subject of cult veneration at Sparta, the antiquity of which may predate her mythological character. In cult practice she was representative of her sex, particularly at adolescence, as were her brothers. Perhaps her chastened image here reflects the influence of Euripides' *Helen* produced in 412 BC.

p. 235   **Athena**: The Greek has *Chalkiokos*; the title of Athena at Sparta (cf. p. 234). At the end of the play she is fittingly celebrated by both Athenians and Spartans. Panhellenic sentiments in the spirit of Lysistrata's speech on p. 227 strikingly conclude the play.

Athena, hail, thou Zeus-born maid: The last four lines of the translation do not exist in the Greek text but have been added on the assumption that the chorus departed singing the praises of Athena as directed by the Spartan. The actual hymn was not included in the text probably because it was a well-known piece and not composed by Aristophanes (cf. the endings of *Ach.*, *Knights*, *Frogs*, *Wealth*).